LEAD
FROM THE
MIDDLE

Mikel Bowman

Copyright © 2023 by Mikel Bowman
All rights reserved.
Printed in the United States of America
Published by Bowman Legacies, LLC
Subject Heading: Leadership

ISBN: 979-8-9892287-1-3

DEDICATION

I want to Dedicate this book to my wife, Anita, who encouraged me to write it. For without her, it would've never happened.

LEAD FROM THE MIDDLE

ACKNOWLEDGMENTS

I am dedicating this book to the love of my life my wife Anita. If it were not for her this book would not have been written.

I want to acknowledge Travis and the gang for helping me through a very difficult situation.

To those who decided to Lead from the Middle and strive to be the change you wanted to see, I commend thee! Your efforts will never return void!

The following names in this book have been changed to protect the identity of those persons.

LEAD FROM THE MIDDLE

FORWARD

As of this writing, there are 57,136 books on Amazon with the word "leadership" in the title. It's fair to ask the question: why do we need one more?

In my opinion, because too few leadership books rest on humility and humanity as the building blocks of solid leadership.

In this book, Mikel Bowman tells the story of two situations of enormous gravity he found himself immersed in – neither of them at his choosing.

In one situation, a living soul hangs in the balance – a son, a brother, perhaps a father; in the other, an entire construction project.

Having known Bowman for some time now, the fact he navigated both of these situations to much-desired results is in no way a surprise to me. Mike is uniquely and naturally gifted to zoom in and then zoom out – context is important in evaluating situations, and with that context Mike sees inside the problem through a deeply empathic lens. His life and his life's work have molded a man of love, honor, and deep respect for others. Mike synthesizes his observations through a prism of faith and humanity while humbly attending to sometimes horrific circumstances for which success seems hardly a consideration, much less a guarantee.

In *Lead From the Middle*, Bowman debunks the notion that only those of high station can affect outcomes. While leadership titan, John Maxwell, de-mystifies leadership in a way that makes every human being a leader in some way (start where you are; use what you have; do what you can), Bowman's practical application in this book provides not only examples of this leadership simplicity, but also a framework to screen one's responses to challenges big and small.

Having witnessed Mike's impact firsthand with our crew, these stories and their delivery represent so much of what is missing in leadership today. His presentations with our crews typically end with red, watery eyes – the good tears – and when you read this book you'll know why.

Mike stitches together teamwork, camaraderie, humility, and respect for others with a work ethic and examples of leadership that create the backbone of successful group effort. His posture is from a place of love – heartfelt, but direct – and it's from this position he gains incredible traction in *Leading From the Middle*.

One of our core values at Sargent is Winning in the Field.

Bowman shows you how.

Herb R Sargent
President/CEO
Sargent Corp

LEAD FROM THE MIDDLE

TABLE OF CONTENTS

	Acknowledgments…………	i
1	A Late Phone call………………	Pg 11
2	Where it all began………………	Pg 15
3	The Juggernaut…………………	Pg 19
4	The Plan & the Problems………	Pg 31
5	The Rally……………………	Pg 45
6	The Everyday………………….	Pg 51
7	Get in the Dirt!...........................	Pg 59
8	What I Didn't Do………………	Pg 67
9	What I Did Do…………………	Pg 89
10	A Line in the Sand…………….	Pg 113
11	I'm Bought In, Now What?………	Pg 129
12	One Chance ……………………	Pg 141

What Not to Do………………Pg 152

What To Do…………………Pg 154

Book Recs relisted……………Pg 157

Bowman Legacies website……Pg 159

About the Author……………Pg 161

LEAD FROM THE MIDDLE

1
A LATE PHONECALL

It is 3am and my phone rings. I kept it next to my bed because of the nature of my job, the General Manager of a booming company that stretched from coast to coast. At this hour, I know the call is one of two scenarios: spam, or one of our California crews. They wouldn't call at this hour unless there was an emergency, so I picked up as soon as I saw the area code. Yup it's one of ours. Wiping the sleep from my eyes and answer with a groggy, "Hello, Mikel here. What's up?"

There is no immediate answer. But it's not silent on the other end of the phone either. My ear is trained to listen for what most folks don't hear and immediately there were some glaring noises in the background that stood out.

The sound of an industrial A/C unit, more than one kicking on and off, I could hear the rain, and a grown man sobbing. Having not programmed all our guys' numbers in my phone yet, I didn't know who it was, but was keenly aware this person was in distress and for whatever reason, decided to call me.

Treading lightly, "Hello? Hey buddy. It's gonna be ok. I'm not going anywhere, and I don't care about the time. I'm here for you. What's going on? Talk to me."

A tearful voice on the other end replies and I must take care to lean into the phone and strive to hear the quiet tones. "I can't do this anymore." More sobbing. "I can't do this, I'm going to kill myself, I have a pistol and I'm gonna shoot myself, Mike. If you call 911, and I see the cops I'll shoot myself right away. You're not talking me out of it and that's not why I called. I'm where no one can find me, and you are about the only person I could think of in this World that actually loves and cares about me. I wanted to say goodbye."

Immediately, I put my caller on speaker phone, and began texting a few trusted guys on the crew. Text: "Dude, I think William is in trouble. I'm talking to him right now. He has a gun and he means business. He won't tell me where he is and swears if he sees the cops, he'll shoot himself right away. But I am pretty sure he is in the AC units behind the pool area close to his apartment. Dude, get en route NOW!" One of the guys texted back, "On my way!", and I replied. "Be careful!"

As an avid outdoorsman I could hear, against all the background noise and sobbing, the all too familiar sound of a semi-automatic handguns' slide engage and a live round jacked in the barrel. Then the sobbing voice, still talking became muffled as the muzzle of that pistol was placed in his mouth. I knew time was of the essence and waiting for the cops would be a death sentence for this guy.

Just by listening I knew right away that he had taken great pains to hide where his body was to lay. He was in a place where the shot would be muffled. Close to a busy highway, tucked far from prying eyes. I could hear that he was in an industrial air conditioner yard. Typically, large AC units are hidden from view with high fences or block walls. I thought of the layout of his apartment complex, having had stayed there for several weeks before. He was going to a place where no one could see. This was not a moment to get attention. This, my friends, was his final stand and he wanted to say goodbye to the one person he thought cared about him: Me!

After 20 years of management experience, and seven years of counseling for the non-for-profit space, I knew this person meant business. I could hear it. I have been here several times before with others. Many will reach out, not intending to actually go through with it, but you cannot gamble on that notion. Every plea you must take very seriously. In my mind this person had already checked all the boxes.

In that moment, that single moment, whatever I said next would mean life or death for someone who was in desperate need. Beyond a shadow of a doubt, whatever I choose to say would be received by someone at the end of their rope. He had to know it was the absolute truth. If I bullshitted this guy for even a moment, it was over, and I had a front row seat.

Before I tell you the rest of the story, let me set the stage for you on what brought us to this fateful moment at 3am, fighting for a good man's life.

2
WHERE IT ALL BEGAN

Years prior to this moment, I noticed a man posting on LinkedIn that piqued my interest. At the time, I was working for a drilling company in the mining industry. In the first year at that company, I was a driller running equipment. Then in year two, a position opened up for the Safety Director, serving our drillers and mechanics, spanning a region of about six states in the Midwest. (Missouri, Illinois, Kentucky, Tennessee, Indiana, Ohio).

I had come to a place where the current job was in a good place and I had the hang of it. But that was the thing. Though I was making a difference, though I really cared for the guys I worked with, though I knew that I was doing good work, I was no longer challenged. There was just nowhere to go from where I was. I felt stuck, and heading into my fifth year, I was feeling a bit stagnant and ready for some change.

These LinkedIn posts were refreshing compared to the usual chit chat that we were seeing online. He was challenging leaders to rise up and do more for their employees, he was giving the charge to fight against cultural norms, he was waving the flag to usher in a higher sense of worker responsibility and servanthood. This guy was speaking my language in every post. His posts were full of leadership goodies and solid business culture that I could not help but to repost, and comment on.

Before long, my online banter back and forth with the young President had become more serious, and he asked me if I was open to a conversation. On our first call, he offered me a job on the low-end executive level of his organization. I told him, "Look brother. I'm a Safety Director of a drilling company, not an Exec. I come from the non-for-profit space before this, and before that the blue-collar world. I still drill at times and help out turning a wrench if need be. I'm not afraid of getting dirty, so I'm not sure I'm what you are looking for. I'm not sure I am exec material. I'm also not willing to lay down and not fight for our guys in the field. Execs haven't a clue what's going on out here in the field, and they write policy and set expectations that prove it. Look brother, I like what you're selling but I'm not going to make you promises or present myself as something I am not. Thanks for the offer but No."

This went on for almost a year. I'll never forget his last

pitch. "Look man, you have integrity. You know how to lead. We're in your back yard. You'll see your kids more. You'll be home more. I get it that you aren't an exec, I get that you aren't willing to present yourself as something that you're not. But I see untapped potential in you, and I believe your boss hasn't a clue how to tap into it. I do! We need good people; we'll figure out the rest as we go. Just have coffee with me. Let's sit in the same room, hear me out, then you can say no to my face."

Ok, now you tell me what's a guy supposed to say to that, No? Arrogantly I said, "Ok, bring your spreadsheets, I want to see your financials. I want to see your business plan, your prospects, I want to know what debt you are leveraging, and what I'm working with. I want to see what jobs you have going on. I want to know who all is involved." His reply, "I'll have it for you at Starbucks, Saturday morning, first thing!" I thought to myself, 'Well crap! Now I have to go and meet this guy.'

Saturday came around and I showed up in my work truck. He was late. He was always late. I dare say he probably is still late. Late irks me to no end. I was definitely saying No. Who shows up late to a meeting they set up? Especially after all the times you've tried to have the meeting? Even though he was late, even though I had convinced myself that I would say no, at the end of one large black coffee and our conversation, I was hooked, sold, on board, drinking the Kool-Aid, and any other saying you can think of.

I don't know if it was the caffeine rush that made me say yes or his obvious passion for people, and striking out against an old, stale industry, that made me drop my guard. Either way, before I knew it the word yes was coming out of my mouth quicker than I could grab it! When I said yes, the man actually gave me a hug! His face lit up like a Christmas tree! "You just made my whole day!" His exuberance was electric, and I must admit, I miss having him in my life, just for his ability to inspire others, and his childlike excitement when things went his way. There's no one on this planet that can get you jazzed up and self-confident like he could. I truly believe he could sell a torch to a man on fire!

I immediately called my wife and said, "Well, I don't know how this happened, but I just said yes to this job and I'm in my truck scared to death of what I just agreed to! This guy is either the biggest car salesman I've ever met or an evil genius, and they're probably gonna fire me in a year. Either way, I feel the Lord is in this, and something tells me I need to give it a go!" (I was wrong by the way. Took 'em two years to fire me.)

I was told we were going to do great things! I was told we were going to change the industry! We were gonna fight for the blue-collar people! We were going to be different. With that charge, I couldn't just walk away. I couldn't say no to *that*! I had to see this thing through till the end. This was my chance to fight for the blue-collar-world and the wonderful people in it. I had to say yes!

3

THE JUGGERNAUT

Working for a startup with a solid backing was exciting! There was so much happening all at once that each day presented its own challenges and weeks turned to months more quickly than any other position I had ever held. Looking back, this company was going full throttle for a while and had no signs of slowing down. Jobs kept coming in, as did new employees. Our economy and the need for infrastructural work fever-pitched businesses like us, and it was feasting time! The only catch was getting people in the seats to harvest the feast.

To remedy the need to fill positions we hired a Recruiter, a sweet soul of a woman that we eventually almost broke from the volume of work, and the challenges a fast-moving company with an unintentional approach to leadership will bring. Then we hired another recruiter. We hired a Safety Director, then fired her. Then fired another safety person. Foremen were coming in and out so fast I could no longer keep the names straight. Executive staffers were hired, then fired, and the revolving door had my head spinning knowing it wasn't going to be long that I too would be slung out the door like yesterday's refuse.

Seeing this, the staff began to stress, many were afraid of losing their jobs. Our mantra for the organization: "Be the Change" became more of a crass joke amongst the field staff rather than an inspiration for good culture, as was its original intention. All this is to be expected with a company growing quickly in an industry like mining, which demands more of you as each day passes. As one boss told me, "If you stand still in this industry, you'll get run over!". Unfortunately, it was quickly taking a toll on our workers and quality of work in the field. We were stretched too thin.

On a day like any other, another phone call came from California; a job site that I referred to as 'the Juggernaut'. Not because of the scope of work to be done, but rather for the continued problems we were facing there day to day. We had met so many challenges and it seemed as soon as one was leapt over, another would present itself. On many occasions I flew out to CA to support and get through an issue, only to feel we took ten steps back in the following month or so. At times it felt hopeless that we would ever make this client happy.

When the phone call came in, I was at my desk, and I saw the CEO walk into the president's office. Open-concept offices allow you to hear literally everything, and in their conversation, I heard my name being mentioned. I knew it was only a matter of seconds I would be called in. "Mikel, come here."

My computer was already turned off and packed into my backpack. I knew I would be getting a plane ticket, so I opened the Delta app on my phone, and was looking to book the flight. The CEO told me, "Mikel, site X has a real problem. I'm going to need you to get a one-way ticket to California. (Button pressed; Flight booked) We've got two shifts out there and Frank is in a froth and threatening to kick us off the site." The president looked up from his desk. This guy never seemed rattled. No matter what we faced, even if he were mad, he kept a good attitude and a professional stance. "Mikel, if we fail here, we've failed as a company." No pressure, right? Even with all of this drama, neither of these young leaders were in a state of panic. They weren't freaking out, they were simply stating what needed to happen, and the way they handled things, I have a tremendous respect for.

Now, let me map out the issues for you, starting with the leadership of the site. Not *our* leadership, but rather the one who we, as a contractor, were subject to. We'll call him 'Frank'.

Before continuing, I want to let you know in advance that we're gonna talk more about the problems that we will also remedy in this book. Not to be negative, but because that's just how easy it is to fix a hopeless situation. Hang in there with me, as I give you the full view of just how bad things were, and how practicing my method of leadership consistently can bring great results.

Issue #1 Leadership

To date, 'Frank', the site's superintendent over us, is the worst, most corrosive person who has progressed into a leadership role I have ever encountered in my professional career. In all my years in the blue collar and executive world, I have never met anyone so blatantly obstinate, manipulative, and ignorantly hateful. I am convinced that this story would never have happened, had it not been for Frank. And so Frank, thank you, because I learned so much of what *not to do* from you. I am in your debt for the hard lessons learned.

It was not only our staff who hated him, but the entirety of his own staff as well. On many occasions when striving to fix things at the site, laboring to repair the relationship, I would send guys to fix an issue, only to find out later that our guys didn't even create the problem. His crew did. Frank knew it, we fixed it, and he relished in this kind of continual manipulation. I cannot count the phone calls fielded, the hours, weeks, that were devoted to repairing client relationships based solely upon appeasing this unreasonable tyrant of a man. The word-was-out on the site that if Frank didn't like you, he would go out of his way to get you fired. And if that didn't work, he would make your life a living hell.

The extreme pressure our foreman was under having to deal with this person on a daily basis is hard to fully express. I saw an employee crack right in front of me. He wrenched his hands through his hair and sweat poured down his brow, tear-filled eyes with rage and frustration. "I cannot deal with this guy a second longer. I mean, what the hell is his problem? I've worked at bigger places, done more complicated work. He's never happy!"

We had a regional manager who lived not an hour away from the site, a great human whom I hold in high esteem. This regional manager was no slouch. He knew what he was doing and had proved it a thousand times over, having had run this very site on a previous and much grander scale without failing. But he refused to work there now because of Frank. It was sad to me that Frank had so gotten under this man's skin so much that he couldn't stand to be in the same room with the guy. So much so, our RM wouldn't even darken the door unless he was made to. I mean don't get me wrong, I understood. But it shouldn't have to be this way. The only time he came to check on things was three weeks later when the president of our company made a visit, after all the changes were made and the client was finally happy. I really felt for him and the crew as this kind of leader is the absolute worst. I would rather work with a nicey-nice narcissist than a manipulative brute any day.

One of the bigger problems that this showed me right away, however, was that both the client and our company cared more about money than they did the wellbeing of our people. Still to this day I cannot understand why our president didn't stand up for our workers more. Why he didn't stand up for our regional manager and our foreman and go down the list? This, of course, is the subject of a different book altogether.

Issue #2 Safety

We were being told that we were not doing the job safely enough. And to some degree I can see where they were coming from. Rollovers and safety infractions were rampant, but we weren't the only ones. The site's staff had just as many issues, but we learned early that we weren't allowed to mention it and to keep to ourselves. As a matter of a fact, for two years prior, in all the times I had visited this site, I never once saw their safety director in the field. I can't count how many times one of us would fly over there just to make for certain all was well. I will say that we had a very young staff, and with young staffers comes a litany of emotional, youthful, and irresponsible issues. Many of these kids just didn't see the importance of safety and Frank had good cause to call us on this one. The client stated that he wanted a full-time safety staffer from our company, on each shift. I was elated for this rule, I must admit! With a job this big, a safety presence needed to be there from day one. Lobbying for on several occasions, or trying to mention this in the early days was met with a resounding brush-off. Now that the client demanded it, I was overjoyed, and would make sure we had one for both shifts. So to say the least we had a whole list of things that needed to be worked on.

Issue #3 The Staff

From what we were being told, our team at the site was falling apart. There were clicks and factions. Our guys were falling into the trap of secluding themselves into the cool kids vs the nerds, middle-school mentality that we as adults still tend to gravitate toward. Not only did the site present dangerous issues, not only did the client's management have it out for us, but our own people were also doing things to undermine company leadership. Some strove to manipulate our leaders in order to get other workers kicked off the site or fired just because they didn't like them. Others, it seemed, were vying for favor with the

hopes of moving up the ladder. It seemed from the outside that there was a small group of guys really trying to get along, but without proper leadership, efforts to bring the team together were drowned out by the constant drama of a team gone astray. Like a wild horse without a bit and bridle, they were running wild and breaking fences. There were fist fights happening, talks of vengeance, the aforementioned safety issues and chaos. There were times our team more resembled a chapter from Lord of The Flies, rather than a mine site. Conditions at one point had so deteriorated that a gun was brought on site by one of our people for the purpose of protection, not vengeance. It seems there was a dispute between one of our leaders and a co-worker. Fortunately, nothing happened, and we were able to head-off the situation before it escalated out of control but this was what I was heading into.
Ok, does this map out the site for ya?

    With further investigation I later learned the majority of the staffers at this particular site (leadership included) had put in for a transfer to another site or made complaints to HR about work conditions and issues there. This was a very tell-tale sign that things were not right. When everyone, including leadership, puts in for a transfer, it doesn't take a rocket scientist to figure out that the site had tough demands for meeting its daily challenges. The crucible of a crumbling infrastructure and team that seemed doomed to fail.

Issue #4 Quality of Work

For this situation, I give you the most unbiased opinion I can muster: We were doing a good job considering site conditions and other contractors we had to work with. However, my opinion means very little when the client says, "not good enough." Even though we were exceeding production goals, the client gave us a list to submit to again, and I was more than happy to lend a hand and help get this list accomplished.

Issue # 5 My Directives

1. I was not able to fire, write up or discipline our supervisor in any way because the client liked him.

2. I had no budget and was unable to offer more money to an employee for the safety role. I, as the GM and safety professional, was not allowed to choose the person for the job. I was told one would be picked for me, and our safety director was to work with them.

3. I would not be getting help from our upper management team. Our regional manager refused to work with Frank.

All other staffers were busy at other sites. Looking back, I was not their last choice, I was their only choice!

4. I was not allowed to stand up to the client or point out where they were going wrong. I was not allowed to stand up to our client on behalf of our employees. My directives were to get along with site management and Frank at all costs.

5. It was said to me: "If we fail here, we fail as a company", and also "We have nowhere for the 75 employees at that site to go". So, barring leadership, they would all be going home and not to work elsewhere within the company.

Having been there several times before I must say, the site was no joke. The challenges our staffers met daily were so numerous I cannot even begin to list them all. Not to mention having to deal with Frank. That was one of the biggest challenges. The site was absolutely huge! It was one big hole in the ground. My first visit there I saw a D-9 CAT dozer (for those unfamiliar, a D9 is considered a fairly large dozer.) in the bottom of the pit and it looked like a micro machine! (If you've never heard of micro machines, look 'em up. They're small!) There were so many moving parts to this place, and for our young first-timers it was a daunting task to keep it all in their grasp. From safety challenges to the material harvested, there were a hundred steps to everything.

Having been to this site many times, I'd witnessed two foremen crumble under the pressure of it. We were doing well at most of our other sites but this one was a real thorn in my side. And yet, I must be honest, even with all the drama, challenges, and hardships this place represented, I loved being there! Moreover, for the simple fact that there was so much going on there, and each day presented a new challenge. We had so many fresh faces there and these young men and women had come to us with hopes of making the industry and their lives a better place. No matter what part of the country they came from, no matter shape, size, color, religion, or lack thereof, I adored the kaleidoscope of the human experience that was openly displayed on a daily basis. For me, one who has chosen a profession to help businesses and individuals find the best in themselves and forge ahead, the overall vibe of this place was electric, both good and bad.

4
THE PLAN & THE PROBLEMS

The Plan: Upper management rerouted our current Safety Director, who was on another job, and told her to take the first flight she could find to California. I called her personally and apologized for the last second re-route, but it was for the cause of safety and to keep our guys working. She was a trooper and agreed, though inconvenient she would be there.

The plan was I would work midway through the first shift and stay through the second shift. She would get there the next morning and take the next day shift. Moving forward we'd each work opposite shifts and keep it that way, so as to glean intel from both shifts. Then we would meet for lunch the following day with the head foreman, share said intel, and lay out the plan moving forward. Easy enough, right?

Following are the issues I encountered, entering the site on day one.

Problem 1 Day One: As soon as my plane landed, I rented a truck and headed to the site. Traffic was a breeze, and I got there quickly, signed in and headed up the mountain to our job trailer. Luckily, at the top, I noticed our Lead Foreman's truck parked out front so I headed right in and stepped into his office. He looked up the second I walked through the door, and his face turned bright red and said, "What the hell are you doing here? No one told me you were coming!" I shut the door behind me. He was obviously not happy to see me, and this was not going to be pretty. I sat down in the chair across from his desk. "Brother, I left as soon as I heard." He looked at me with bewilderment. "Heard what?" I was shocked by the statement. Just a few short hours ago I was told all was lost. The sky was falling for heaven's sake! I was told we were about to lose this client. Then when I walk in, our foreman doesn't know why I'm here?!

I trouble shoot. I make things better, smooth things over, make things right! THAT'S WHAT I DO! WHY DOESN'T THIS GUY KNOW WHY I'M HERE! Now I'm the one who's bewildered.

"Well brother, why do you think I'm here?" He looked square at my face and denied knowing why they would send me. Why would they race me out here and not inform the forman that I was on my way? Ok, that's the first issue. <u>He doesn't know that there's a problem.</u> With further probing I came to the following realization: I bought a one-way ticket, rerouted a coworker from an important site, going to miss my daughter's recital, and this guy, the most important hinge point to making things happen, hadn't even been debriefed by the exec team that sent me in the first place.

Furious with upper management, I cannot express my disappointment at that time. I was so angry that they would send me yet again without so much as having a conversation with our leadership team at the site and letting them know that we were on our way to help with the current situation. And to this day I remain bewildered when organizations do not take the time to intentionally set the stage for issues to be resolved. It's astonishing how any company can believe even for a second that resolutions will come to hard problems by just throwing people at them with no real plan. What's even worse? When execs stand there scratching their heads as to why things aren't working out when they act this way. This was most certainly the case, as I stood in front of a very tired job foreman.

Problem #2 Day One: It wasn't long until the second-shift guys showed up, awaiting their trip to the ready line, and the first-shift followed, loading up for their ride home. Both shifts converged in front of the work trailer almost all at once. You would think with that many people meeting at the same place, encompassing a very tight area, there would be a lot of racket. You know the kind. Comrades mocking each other, people chatting about the day, work stuff. But no. No one was chatting. They were all just standing there and many just had their heads down.

Like a fly on the wall, I sat back and wanted to see how the foreman, leads, and other workers interacted. 75 people with as many backgrounds as you can imagine in one spot, and all of them in small groups talking to no one else. No one was crossing party lines, no high fives, no 'go team', just give me your load counts and go home, for the first shift. For the second shift, it was: get in the vans and get to the ready line. No toolbox talk, no new information about site changes, no 'go-give-em-hell boys', nothing! Just get to work.

These guys were divided! Leaderless! Life had become about load counts and production. The human element was all but gone. No real interaction, no teamwork, just another day plodding off like the rest. I was very saddened to see this. With so many great guys on the team you would think at this moment in the day, this place would be humming with excitement. It's work, of course, I know not every day is going to be a joyous event, but to see things so mundane in a group with so much potential, showed how truly worn-down, and under-led, these guys actually were.

Problem #3 Day One : Our leaders were like zombies. They were just going through the motions. Getting paperwork done, getting guys to where they needed to go, jotting down load counts, they weren't happy to be there. It was more than obvious these guys were just trying to get work done and keep their heads down. Everyone was in a rut. There was no team. There was no comradery. Nothing. Just a bunch of individuals trying to make it through another mundane workday. They were mentally checked-out. And that, my friends, is a problem. Checked-out leaders create complacent, disengaged, employees. Complacent, disengaged employees create problems. Lots of them, of which, can be the permanent kind: Death.

I have unfortunately seen this all before. Day after day, load after load, production sheet after production sheet, and guys forget how dangerous our work can be. And it's not long when something bad happens. That's the kind of phone call no leader worth his salt ever wants to get. It is so important that you, as a leader, never check out no matter what the issue is at home or at work. Leaders are the most vital component to the team. We lead the way! We influence! We set the tone! Stay diligent my friends, someone's life may depend on it.

Problem #4 Day Two: I worked through the second shift like a fly on the wall, absorbing everything that was happening. Taking haul truck rides, pickup rides, monitored radio chatter, talked with site supervision and employees, and scanned site conditions. Safety issues were addressed in real time, but I let everything else slide and allowed my people to lead, while monitoring their actions. This is something I did for the first week. Yup. For a whole week I did nothing but show up, watch, listen, mark things for changing and gain trust, but I am getting ahead of myself.

Driving back to my hotel room the next morning at 3:30am west coast time, I had been up for over 24 hours, since 4am eastern the previous morning. I was ready to hit the sack; I am certain my hotel room neighbor heard me snoring. Per the plan, I showed up the next day around noon and there waiting at the site was our Safety Director. She had a big job. I also have to say she was 'good people' too. Our staff were like cowboys really, and compared to what she was accustomed to, it must have seemed as though she had stepped back into the Wild West. You better believe she had a lot to say during lunch! All of which, by the way, was insightful and spot on. Looking across the table I knew she was upset and probably a little bummed she had left a good company for this one. Seeing the scope of all she had to accomplish, and the expectations placed on her shoulders was going to be no small task. Using this time to reassure her, and devise a plan moving forward, by the end of the lunch we were both ready to charge ahead and fix this thing.

Until Frank. Yup, after I had just rallied my General, the enemy came in and stole everything that had been done. There he was, standing tall in all his male-pattern baldness and Beaky Buzzard bravado lurking around the job trailer. He was waiting for us. I saw our Safety Director deflate a little, and I'm certain she saw the same in me.

"Let's talk inside." Just the way he said it you knew we were in for a lulu of a conversation. The three of us, the Foreman in charge, the Safety Director, and myself stood on one side of the work trailer and Frank on the other, pacing like an alley cat. He was charged up and ready to blow. What happened next was 20 minutes of the most unprofessional litany of curse words and blame-shifting I have ever seen in all my career as a Counselor, Miner, GM, Safety Director, and Consultant, combined. Because I already knew how Frank was, and a show was expected, but what we got was so much more. He was mad, but this version of mad was so pathetic at one point I didn't know if I should laugh or be furious. I mean, was this guy joking?

What makes matters worse, he kept pandering bravado like he hadn't done before. Most of his time was spent staring at our safety director. She was tall, bright-eyed and a handsome person, and I realized he was 'showing off' just for her. Could this get any more awkward? Our new Safety Director had never seen Frank in full bloom, so to speak, however she stood tall and unflinching. I was disappointed that she was experiencing this so soon on the job with us. Poor lady didn't have anything to reference. Through the whole thing, she was very professional and poised but obviously, this was not the way to fix problems or break in a new Safety Director.

Knowing full-well that this would really bother her, I was right. After each belligerent rant and four-letter-word came forth from his mouth, fever-pitching himself into a sweaty froth, I could see our Safety Director deflate just a little bit more. She had never been talked to like this before on a job, but she knew we couldn't fight back and like the classy person she was, she stood there strong as an oak and said nothing.

If warranted, we would have understood Frank's rage, but there was no reason for this. Owning your part in any given situation is vitally important, but later I would find out that many of the issues at hand weren't even being done by our staff. Our employees didn't have rollovers at this site. No fender benders. No near misses. To boot, we were meeting production demands.

By the time he was finished I was so furious I didn't know what to do. At one end, our people needed to be defended and I'm not the kind of guy to take things lying down like that. He said things in that room that day that I personally wouldn't allow anyone to get away with. He was crass, vulgar, and to say unprofessional is the understatement of a lifetime. On the other hand, I knew that if I said the wrong thing, I could get us kicked out and a lot of people were counting on us to keep things going smoothly. Our guys had faith in me to make things right and I didn't want my ego or pride to get in the way. My orders were clear. At all costs get along with Frank and fix this. So, I stood there mad as a wet hen and said nothing. Not for Frank's sake, not for the client's sake, but for the sake of our team and my directives.

Once Frank was done, I simply started, "I understand you are angry, Frank. And we are here to strive to fix all that…." Before I could say another word, Frank interrupted, "You haven't done a goddamned thing! You've been here for three days and nothing's changed." Swallowing my wrath, I continued, "Frank, we haven't been here three days. It's barely been two for me, and our Safety Director just got here late last night. This is her first day on the site. We've made many changes on the night-shift already which have been documented and will submit to both you and our management team. And we'll keep making changes until the job is done. It is our expressed desire to make these changes and keep them that way." Frank stood there shaking his hands over his head and ranting belligerent nonsense. "I don't give a fuck what you are here to do! You guys don't have a fucking clue what you are doing! And your boss! That damned president of yours would rather look good than be useful. Where the hell is he now? He should be here! Instead, he sends his lackey. You guys make me sick! It's always the same!" And with that, he marched out.

Folks, I'm no saint. I'm a blue-collar guy through and through. This was very hard for me to take lying down. First off, this was not our only jobsite. Secondly, though we may have had our differences, our President was a very busy, hardworking man. He lived on an airplane; the guy was never home. These issues we were having were common to the industry. No one was hurt, production goals were met, equipment wasn't damaged, and our guys were jumping through every hoop the contract stipulated us to do. Afterwards I had to get off by myself and call a trusted friend who really knows me and get that moment off my chest. I needed to unload that moment because I wasn't there for me, we were there for the men and women of the company we worked for. The bulk of them were good people who had their hope and trust in us to fix things no matter what. We had to take it on the chin if we were going to be successful there. My friend helped me to understand that I was doing the best I could with what I had. (Thank you, Levi!) The other great thing was that I was not alone. Our Safety Director was there with me, and I had her support. With that, and a plan already in action I knew we were well on our way to find a solution.

That night I had the privilege of having dinner with our Safety Director and her boyfriend. We hadn't met before and I have to say, he was a really good egg. He had come up to see her as she had been away from home for some time, before coming out here. He had concerns about his significant other, and in contrast to our day, we kept the conversation light. After dinner, I headed back to the jobsite, and they went to their hotel. Calling my wife on the way, I predicted, "Five-will-get-you-ten, our Safety Director won't be back tomorrow." I was betting on it.

Problem #5 Day Three: The next day I arrived just in time to catch the second shifters heading up to the ready line. Entering the job trailer I asked where my right-hand safety person was, and sure enough, the foreman had the same question. "I haven't a clue where she is. She didn't come in this morning." My first thought was worry. Maybe she was sick. Maybe she had an issue I wasn't aware of. Which can hit you when you work traveling jobs. Our hotel wasn't The Ritz and I wanted to make for certain that she was safe, first and foremost. Come to find out, first thing that morning the sweet couple loaded up and headed home, telling no one. I can't say what that conversation was like between them, but I imagine it went something like:

"Babe, you're coming home with me or I'm going up that mountain with you tomorrow. No one, and I mean no one talks to you like that. No job is worth this kind of treatment."

I am certain, had that been *my* wife, I would have done much the same for her. She would have been escorted home and dared somebody to say something about it. Seeing them together, you could tell that he loved her like that. This is probably similar to how it went down. As I said before, I could see this coming anyway. Even telling my wife the day before that our Safety Director was probably going to leave. I just didn't think it would be this quickly. Immediately, the exec team was made aware of the issue and they then informed me, no one else would be en route. Day three, and I was officially alone.

Now this is the point where I tell you that I was a beast and didn't care. This is the part where I tell you the issues at hand had no bearing on my emotions and I was as steady as a man with all the confidence in the world. Bullshit! I was enraged! I had no support, no authority, and now, no help! What was I supposed to do? My directives, the few vague ones that were given, stated that as GM I was to facilitate the best I could *with the Safety Director*. Other than to go and fix it, that was all I had to go on. I knew not to get resentful because that would never move the needle. These guys needed my help. Most of them had more experience than me. What could I bring to the table that would change anything at all?

Stepping outside, I prayed. Centering myself, I knew that I had to make this work. My back was up against the wall. At that time, I already felt I was no longer bringing the kind of value to the company that was necessary to keep me employed. On borrowed time, I needed to make a homerun. But more than that, there were 75 folks who thought I was here to fix everything. Oh, wait… I was! That considered, there was no plan B for me. It was time to burn the boats, so to speak. Win here or I knew it would be marching orders, both for myself and many others. Not only that, but for me personally, when folks need help, I want to be the guy who is there. I want to be one who adds to the solution and not to the problem. So, it was time to put away my frustration and look for the solutions. I had been to this site several times, and several of the guys and I had become very close. I was fighting for them as well. They were all relying on me to make things happen and not just put a Band-Aid on things and roll. This time, that wasn't going to work. All I knew clearly at that moment was what *not to do*.

My friends, isn't that half the battle?

5
THE RALLY

After a few days on the site, I was sitting on a boulder as the crews came in, ready to switch shifts. Per usual everyone there was camped out in their little islands secluded from the other groups. We had the cowboys, the cool guys, the wanna-be's. We had the religious outcasts, the inner-city guys, and the loners. The foreman walked past them all as if they didn't exist. I had had enough! I stood up and climbed up on the steps of the job trailer and hollered to the crew. "Gentlemen gather around! I want to talk to you about something that I see that needs to change if we are to progress any further as a company, as a team, and for you young people." Immediate awkward silence. "I said, gather in! That means come closer, I've got something to say!" You could tell these guys hadn't come together for a single thing. I knew I had two types of people in this audience, and how they would react to what I was about to say.

One was the kind who were open to and who knew they needed a change at the site. The second was the kind who liked the mundane, or reveled in dissension, making problems, and dividing people according to a myriad of pathetic reasons. I don't tolerate that kind of mess on my sites or in my life. If you're reading this, and you are that kind of person, throw my book away, hell burn it for all I care. But, if you are the kind of person who really wants to learn to lead and are hoping for more for your life: Read on my friend!

The guys stood there in front of me waiting to receive another butt-chewing and I could see the dead expression on their faces. I had been there with them at several points in my own life. I knew how they felt. They were on a losing team, they were all ready to leave, and they were resolved to be defeated.

"I've been here for several days and have witnessed a lot of things and instead of chewing everyones' butts for what we know we are doing wrong, I wanted to see for myself before making assumptions coming in here with guns a-blazing. I wanted to hear what you all had to say, and give you guys the chance to speak. What I have witnessed is more good than bad. But the one thing I see that is killing our progress here is that you all have put yourselves in your own little groups and isolated the team into little sections. Some of you have even gone so far as to plot against teammates you don't like or stand in their way of moving ahead. You make fun of each other, you talk behind one another's backs, some of you suck up to management to get ahead, you argue, you dislike one another for your differences. My friends, we are a kaleidoscope of colors, sizes, religions, and beliefs. I can pick a million-and-one things that separate us or point out why we are all different. Isn't that the way society has it for us as well? Our whole World is on fire right now! As I look at all of your faces looking back at me, I can see clearly that this has been a rough site to work at. You are tired. You are fed up! And yet you, as a dissected team, have met production goals *consistently*. You've been crushing it! Imagine what we can do together as a cohesive team! Look outside this mine site. The whole world is fever pitched to thwart one another, complaining about this group or that and our nation is more separated now than it has been in a long time. Even so, that doesn't have to be us! We can be the change! We can be the difference! We can be the example to the rest of the world that here, right here with this company we can be strong together! When you step on our site we should think as one, we should move as one, and we should fight as one!

So many of you are looking out only for yourselves and it disturbs me knowing we could be so much more! All of us are so different and yet we have one thing in common: We all work at the same place. We all run the same equipment. And many of you sleep in the same apartments. So tell me why do we look more like a bunch of middle schoolers instead of a fucking wolf pack! I've ridden with one-percenter bikers. I was never a part of a club, but I buried a few, as a pastor. They allowed me into their world because of it and the things I learned from them is this: When you ride for the patch, you have the protection of the pack! Everyone has to pull their weight, and by god, you look out for one another even if you don't like each other. Because you have one thing in common, you ride for the brand!

Well, that's what I want for us and from this day forward this is my expectation. You will get along. I will no longer tolerate the childish squabbles you guys are having on site or at the apartments. Stop the adolescent picking on and making fun of one another. If someone doesn't like it, knock it off! Resolve your issues like adults or get off my site. If you need help doing that, I would be glad to do so. From here on out, you will look out for one another both on and off this site. If I hear another negative comment on the radio when someone points out a safety issue to you, I will write you up immediately. If I find out the same thing happens in your apartments, I'll send you home.

The 'buddy system' is dead in this way. I will not tolerate putting favorites or buddies ahead of those who have merit and come to work faithfully and do their jobs without complaining. These are the people I will push to the forefront! Every man here will be judged upon their merit. So for those of you that have been corrosive, slacking, or haughty, because the foreman is your pal, I'll be watching you. I don't care how cool you think you are, I do not care how chummy we get, I don't care about how much you think you know. I want to see how much you care. And if you're that kind of person, I will go out of my way to help you. What you don't know we can help you learn.

I make this my promise to you. I am here to help you both on this site and off. If for any reason you need someone to talk to, about personal or work issues I will support you providing they are not in the production time of your shift. I also promise if there is a safety concern, I will immediately stop what I am doing and help assist in any way that I can.

When I look at you, looking back at me, I see greatness in all of you. (Someone rolled his eyes and huffed) I saw you roll your eyes brother, but I actually mean it! I see greatness in you, and I'll be damned if I'm not here to help you and others find, hone, and grow it. But I'll only be here a short while and that greatness is *up to you* to enhance beyond my stay. Though I see it, that in and of itself is not enough. It's up to you if you want to make it shine brighter. And with that greatness you can shine individually, but I would rather shine together as one! Now I have my orders and promises to you. If I fall short of that, hold me accountable as I will the expectations I have for you. Is anyone here unable to comply, or have any issues with what I just said? If not, then let's get first-shift home and second: get to work."

No one spoke. They all just stood there looking back at me like I had just pooped a monkey out of my butt, and it was dancing a jig while begging for change right in front of them. At first, I must admit the silence was staggering. I thought I had really flubbed it but the response afterwards was affirming that the nail was hit right on the head! Seldom do I get that many slaps on the back or side comments after I speak. This time around was uplifting. So many of the people came to the side and told me how much it meant to them that I was there and that they already saw a difference in morale and work environment. So many of our crew scheduled time to chat with me about their careers and personal issues.

That all sounds great, but the fact is, it overwhelmed me because I knew if I didn't deliver consistently, the idea that solid trust would be formed was an impossibility. So the challenge was set on both sides of the management team and it was time to walk it out.

6
THE EVERYDAY

<u>Leading from the Middle is not:</u> an easy fix. It takes time, consistency, intentionality, patience, and determination.
<u>Leading from the middle is not:</u> Giving one fancy speech and everything changes over night.
<u>Leading from the Middle is:</u> a way of doing business, leading others, and living life. Once you take the helm of this kind of lifestyle you will indeed have your ups and downs. There will be times of living it to the T, and days where you slack, later realizing you fell off the path. That's to be expected. Just get back on the path. It's as simple as that.

The following are several small things that were done that added up to big change. I want you to know that pacing yourself is pertinent. And again remember that consistency, and quality of your leadership approach is much more important than fancy speeches or pumping people up.

From what the exec team told me about our clients' expectations, I had about three weeks to fix this site. It also seemed from the writing on the wall, that my job depended on success. For me however, the bigger bummer was that after I left the site, the current leader would most likely revert to his old ways, and it would be back to miserable business as usual as there was no one to hold him accountable. So the whole things seemed so futile.

Knowing this going in, made it difficult for me at the onslaught. But once my ego got put aside it was easier for me to get focused on the job at hand.

What must be understood, the former Forman was, for the most part, well-liked amongst the staff. However, he was promoted to a new position and replaced with someone that most of the team resented. I hated that for the new foreman, but he made matters worse by leading in a consistently corrosive way. I made the attempt to show him how to lead, but for the most part he kept his distance from me, and often took pains to avoid me altogether. If I could not influence or demand change from him, I knew I had to go another route.

So why go to the extent of leading this way at all, if another leader can come in and change everything? Easy. Because it's the right thing to do, that's why. And anything worth doing, is always worth doing right. As I had mentioned before, there were 75 guys who were counting on me to keep them working. That alone, my friend, meant a lot to me.

After I knew that I was alone, I had to be strategic about my approach to the plan to move forward. The lead foreman wasn't my biggest fan, and the site super hated me. It was time to start somewhere. And that 'somewhere' rested in the site assistant foreman: 3 on day shift, 2 on night shift, including the night shift lead foreman. So often when we need to lead, we look at the whole picture and get overwhelmed. I understand, I am quick to do that as well. However, when we realize there are certain roadblocks or dead ends like in this situation, we need to immediately look at what we can do instead of obsessing on all the things we cannot. Then, be quick to get after the things you can do. You'll be surprised at what a difference that can make in a pinch.

I took a lot of truck rides with these five guys. And these truck rides didn't consist of just riding around and doing nothing. That's the trap a lot of execs get into. They go to the site, slap a few Band-Aids here and there, ride around in the truck and bolt. For change to be lasting, we have to double-down on being intentional about EVERYTHING! So, for me, the truck rides were a vital source of intel. No matter where you are at, whether at home, the office, or the site, my truck ride might be your office, their office. This concept applies and can be adapted to any leadership situation.

These rides with the foreman were also a vital time to get them on the same page as to how we would be approaching our new leadership style and set the kind of standard that they would follow. Remember, you can't do this alone.

First and foremost, my head was on a swivel for site condition issues. The more I rode around, the more I got to know every nook and cranny of the site, and in doing so, I was more than able to catch safety concerns, or housekeeping issues by being out there with the troops. Gradual changes made every day to impact efficiency, adds up.

Secondly, after a day or two, the foreman began to trust me. They would witness me shoveling out tracks, or taking out the trash, cleaning out their truck trash, and pouring into our entry level guys and filling them with hope. This would tighten the bonds with my guys and before long they would be sharing every gory detail of home life and work life in such a way that gave me proper intel to make rational decisions.

Thirdly, our entry level guys were all over the place. This gave me the opportunity over just a few days to get to know the entire staff and make solid opportunities to tighten the bond with them and let them see I not only cared about them, but I knew what I was doing, as well. When I needed to make a quick change, when I saw a safety issue, they were quick to pivot and fix whatever I needed because they knew full well that I was there to help.

Lastly, by getting in the dirt with my people, you will be able to see the talent you had in real time. What I found was astounding. There were guys on the site stuck in haul trucks all because our site foreman didn't like them. The reason why he didn't like them was because they held him accountable to cultural and leadership issues. An employee named James was a leader through and through. A former Marine, he was being wasted and shoved to the side all because he wasn't willing to stand aside when bad things were happening. We had another young man who was an absolute wizard at numbers and keeping track of what trucks needed and what services from our vendors. He wasn't liked because he often corrected the foreman when he was wrong. A Hawaiian young man who had foreman written all over him was looked over merely because he was so young. A young woman was looked over because she was married and outspoken. I chose her as our safety lead. Her husband worked for us as well. They both came from coal, they both understood safety, and they both were hard working honest people.

After getting the foreman on board with the way we would lead, we intentionally invested in all of them! We strove to support them in what they needed daily, and we worked through the issues by making them a part of the solution. We went with their plans, allowed them to fail, helped them to see the bigger picture, and poured into them the best virtue and leadership lessons learned along the way to the very best of our ability. Also worth mentioning, with each truck ride we made sure to invest in those people and reach out to them pointing out over the radio (so others could hear) how great a job they were doing, how their efforts affected the team as a whole, and how thankful we were for their hard work. This set an unspoken expectation for what we were looking for in a leader. The whole team got to hear it.

We repeated these actions every single day providing there wasn't a meeting fire to put out. Consistency is what you are looking for. I know I have already said this to you but it's worth repeating. Too many leaders get off to a great start then allow the stresses of everyday life to slow their progress or stifle it all together. When I say every day, I mean *every day*. You see my friend, I didn't just take truck rides and cash it in. I didn't just make it look good. I had a reason for everything and so should you.

If you aren't the owner of the business, but you know you have a failing team, you can still be intentional about how you conduct yourself and inspire others to rise above. Invest time! My friend Herb Sargent says, 'Invest Attention' Instead of 'Pay Attention'. Investing in something/someone brings a return, and investing in your team will bring a return worth the investment. At the same time, you will be growing leaders who will help make every function work better.

Praise people when they do well. Congratulate your teammates for milestones and wins. Help your teammates to consider new pathways for personal and leadership growth. Be the one who is willing to listen to their ideas and help implement them. Then give them credit for the win. Do your best to get involved instead of just keeping your head down and managing your area. Don't feel you have to do it all at once! Little by little, effort after intentional effort, it all adds up. What you will find in the end is strong bonds and lasting friendships. Not only that, but you'll also have a team that is more determined to win together. And that my friend breeds a winning culture time and time again.

LEAD FROM THE MIDDLE

7
GET IN THE DIRT

In many of the jobs I've worked, I've turned out to be more of a fireman than whatever my title was supposed to be. We can't count how many times I called my wife and asked her to pack my bags for me, because as soon as I got home, I would be headed out again to fix something at a site. As far away sites were concerned, I would pick up my rental truck and set out for the apartments or hotels the guys were staying in. In California our guys had apartments. When headed there, I would call someone on the team and ask if it were possible to couch it for several days in their apartment.

In one particular apartment I stayed in, the moment you entered the door you were in the kitchen. Straight away you could see the double doors to the balcony. On the left was the master bedroom with its own bath and balcony, and on the right, two more rooms with a full bath between them. They were nice places to stay. Just past the kitchen was the living room with one armchair and a couch, that would be my bed for the next several days. What a comfy couch it was! (Read: Sarcasm) More like the Edmond Fitzgerald of couches. Sunken and legendarily uncomfortable!

When I had hatched this plan to stay with the guys and see what daily life was like, several of the exec team scolded me. "There are plenty of decent hotels and even better Airbnb's in San Jose. Some even closer to the site than where you are staying. It makes zero sense to stay on a couch with the guys." They couldn't be more wrong. You can't imagine the intel you will get from those dinners, or just hanging out with the crew in their elements. After a few days of hanging out right where they lived, I heard all kinds of dirty little secrets that gave me the heartbeat of what was going on. Most leaders would have never been willing to sleep on a couch, eat dinner from a crock pot with a bunch of miners, sit and hang out after a long day at work, buddy seat it in bumpy equipment, or clean out the trash. And most leaders never really get to the bottom of their real issues, either. Things like who-was-sleeping-with-who on the site. How is this vital, you ask? Internal strife very often happens with romantic relationships and can be a complete powder keg if you are not careful. I'm not saying people can't fall in love, or lust, all I'm saying is that folks need to keep it professional, or chaos ensues.

I found out about safety issues they didn't report to our safety director. How the site management wouldn't put light plants in the darkest parts of the pit. As a matter of a fact, visibility at night was very low in some of the most dangerous parts of the pit. Oh, and there was more. Much, much more! I heard about corrosive employees, and leadership. I already knew Frank was bad, but there were employees who never left middle school in the way they handled new people, or those who maybe didn't fit in. People were getting isolated the moment they got off the plane. Eagerly, they told me all about how our exec staff gave little to no support to helping our foreman handle the daily riggers of leadership, onboarding, training, and teamwork. And it showed in every area of the organization. I was made aware that there was a big drug problem on the site. The guys were drinking too much but that's not all, some were using illicit drugs and were crafty about how they dodged random drug tests. I had the whole site tested and several tested positive for cocaine.

    I took haul truck rides, monitored the cut, dug out tracks, helped maintenance, conversed with the dealer's mechanic, watched the ready line, went on breaks with the guys, took out the trash, listened like a fly on the wall all the while collecting hard data. Just by getting in the dirt with our people, by living life as they did day to day, we can learn the answer to every question our executive team has. This way of leading, *from the middle*, will gain you access to the front seat of your team's culture in such a way that you will get laser beam focused on the answers rather than scratching your head at what the problem is. Consider this, working for that same company I realized in less than a year, more than $80,000 was spent on onboarding, and offboarding alone. This is just time spent hiring and firing. When you add in the recruiters' time, when you consider HR's time vested, when you consider drug tests, paperwork, flights, hotels, direct deposit, training, and the list goes on, the costs soared well over a hundred thousand in a very short time. For some larger companies, these costs range into the millions and they don't even count the cost as they are too busy thinking about production.

Most of the issues pertaining to folks getting fired or leaving to go home boiled down to poor leadership and the chaos that ensues because of people willingly dropping the ball. So why go there at all? Why not lead in such a way that you no longer look at your employees as metrics or units to measure success by? Why not simplify your process in such a way that you truly get to the bottom of what the problem really is. Then prioritize and execute until the problem is solved. It's truly as simple as that.

A young executive told me a story about how they were getting ready to fire just about everyone at another office location. That is, until he himself went there to figure out what the problem was. At first, he was pissed at all the short falls, miscommunications, and all-around failures their western office was seeing. Until he stayed with them for longer. I loved his exact quote, "I was ready to fire them all, until I went out there and camped out for longer than a week. After that, I wanted to fire everyone back home in the Main office!"

You see, he had to get in the dirt with his people. He needed context before making a knee jerk decision. Though his job wasn't in the *actual dirt*, the concept is the same. He needed to experience everyday with his people in order to truly know how to serve them. He needed intel before casting his judgment. After having those things, he was able to make real decisions that mattered, and would bring lasting change. Leading this way may take some time, and time is money, but think of all the money he saved by actually getting in the dirt with his people. If this young man had fired everyone in the western office, think of the severance packages, the paperwork fielded by HR, the time spent in exit interviews, fielding replacements, training them and the time it takes to get the new hires speaking the organization's language. Good Lord! This will be a year of deficit, and unproductive maneuvering that I have personally gone through. You lose a lot of ground when you build a business in this way.

    Issues you face aren't always so obvious as staff issues. All because the organization has a problem doesn't always mean leadership is doing their job to train, mentor, and guide their employees. All because there are issues doesn't mean someone's head needs to be on a chopping block. Most of the time it's much deeper when good employees are vested but not performing, there's always a deeper reason. Especially if they are culturally sound, you need to fight to keep them, considering today's markets. That being said, I knew the problems this site was facing were mounting daily. I also knew that these problems could not be solved by me alone. So, each time I got in the dirt, each time I made a visit, I made for certain to listen, prioritize and execute. No judgment. No yelling. No brow beating or guilt trips. Just encouragement, engagement, and good old-fashioned, consistent leadership. Was it hard? Gut wrenchingly so. Was I away from home a lot that year? Did I miss my family, and wish I was a dad in the mix? You bet! I will say however, modern technology helps make all that easier these days, with facetime and the like. During this time my boss offered to send my wife out to see me. Such a nice thing to do, however, this site was so bad I did not need that kind of distraction, number one. Number two, the guy peeing on the stair landing of my hotel who also slept there every night, wasn't something I wanted my wife to experience! Even though it was hard, it was well worth it to see solid leadership principles at work making a difference.

In order to break through culture issues, in order to achieve that goal, in order to fight social norms, in order to get to that fitness goal, things are bound to be hard. All we have to do is count the cost and be determined to see it through and I'm certainly glad we did. Though all seemed hopeless for a time, to watch things unfold the way they did was a wonderful sight indeed. By the end of week one, I could already see the difference in the leadership staff of the site. They walked lighter, laughed more, and were in the field more. Week one! That was the hope we needed to keep going! To see these guys start to laugh again was the first clue that we as a team were making a difference. To see them be uplifted and joking around instead of the dead eyed complacent workers I had seen the week before filled me and the foreman with motivation to keep forging ahead.

All these guys needed was hope. That's it! The rest would work itself out in time with intentional leadership. But hope, my friends, is almost always the answer. That and bringing a solid attitude to everything you touch will be the catalyst to set the rest of your team's issues into a forward motion. All too often we get bogged down in the issues in front of us and allow ourselves to be drawn down to the level of those problems. Oh, it is subtle at first, but if we aren't diligent to keep our mindsets in a forward moving attitude, we will surely follow the heavy stream of negativity daily life, and others around us can bring. So be vigilant my friends!

8
WHAT I DIDN'T DO

There I was, alone. No support. No one from the executive team would be there to help me in real time. So, what do I do? How do I fix this? Can I fix this? There were guys on that site that had more mining experience, more leadership and management roles, college degrees and certifications than you could shake a stick at. Why would they want to listen to me? Why would they take my advice? How would I even put a dent in a problem this big when no one was coming to the rescue? How would I be able to convince 75 employees, 4 foremen, 1 lead foreman, and a tyrannical superintendent to get along, strive for solutions in a professional manner and work cohesively together as a team? I'll tell you how. By knowing what 'not to do'. The following was a system I put in place years ago when leading people out of issues in their personal lives. I will share that with you now.

1. **I Didn't Yell: (**Don't yell, threaten, or belittle)

This is a much bigger concept than what you may realize. You may hear "I didn't yell" and think, 'Well no duh Bowman, what's that gonna solve?', and I get it. Let's take a deeper dive in the concept of yelling.

When I began my career in non-for-profit, 1on1 counseling would be a part of my duties. Having mentored people before, I felt that I was well-equipped for the task at hand. Boy was I wrong!

I didn't yet have a system of approaching people's personal issues and would jump right in there and start making assumptions right away based on what I thought I already knew. What I didn't know is that a lot of the time people don't know why they do certain things. And if you are going to get into someone's head, you have to gain trust. That my friends, is what it's all about: Relationships first. Especially if you want lasting, consistent change.

By yelling, or being in someone's face about things, they tend to put up a wall between you that will take even longer to tear back down. And we don't want to just climb over these walls. We want to tear them down. In order to do that, we must figure out how they were built, to begin with. Fact is, to make any problem go away, you have to diagnose why it is there in the first place. In order to diagnose problems well, one must be intentionally respectful.

So, telling my team 'how bad they suck' wasn't an option. Also worth noting, Frank was already telling them how much they sucked every day. They didn't need to hear that from me. Then, like Frank, I would be seen as an adversary, instead of an ally who is there to help.

Consider a time when your kids, or staff member has told you, 'Stop yelling at me' when you haven't raised your voice? There's something in that, you know. Yelling is much more than the tonality of your voice, or the use of curse words. It's all about your intention and people are more aware of this than you realize. They feel it. They can tell your intention, not just by the tone of your voice, but also by the content of your words and your character. All the brow beating, all the smart-ass remarks, all the bravado in the world wasn't going to fix this problem and it won't fix yours!

So put yelling aside, be intentional in your conversations, be respectful in your approach, and be aware of the trust wall that you are trying to remove, so you can move forward towards a solution that works for both of you. By the way, this tactic works both at home *and* on the jobsite!

Side Note: For me personally yelling is not the last resort. It is never the resort. Fact is, great leaders lead their own emotions. And if an employee, or an issue has pushed you to start threatening, browbeating, bullying, or yelling, you have come to the end of your skill set and knowledge. And because of this you, yes YOU, have allowed those aforementioned issues to cause you to lose control or act out of turn. You, as a leader, should be held to a higher standard. And even if those above you aren't, you should have the integrity and honor to hold yourself to a higher standard.

Great leaders don't need to yell. Great leaders don't need to 'chew someone's ass'. Great leaders don't need to lose control. Yelling is merely a fear response for feeling like you are losing control of a situation, or person. Control is an illusion. Stop leading from a fear-based mind and progress. You owe it to the people you follow.

<u>Great leaders are:</u>

1. Poised
2. Passionate
3. Patient
4. Honorable
5. Honest
6. People Of Strong Resolve
7. Have Self Control
8. Trustworthy
9. Consistent
10. Self-Aware
11. Transparent
12. Respectful
13. Fair
14. Grateful
15. Understanding
16. Unwavering
17. Influential
18. Courageous
19. Accountable
20. Loyal

Nowhere in that list does it say:

1. Mean
2. Backbiting
3. Gossiping
4. Anxious
5. Vengeful
6. Liar
7. Yeller
8. Threatening
9. Condescending
10. Manipulative
11. Reactionary
12. Short Tempered

Of the attributes of what a good leader should be, (1-20), many will say no one person can have all those. But I will tell you undoubtedly, you could not be more wrong. I've met those kinds of leaders, I've worked with them, I've been mentored by them, the kind that really are striving for more. Oh, they weren't a blinding success the day they started their career. Of course not! It may have taken them years to get to the place where others checked boxes 1-20 when asked about their leader's character.

The moment we realize that we have a passion for people and want to strive to help them rise above and win, you will no doubt begin a lifelong journey to see where you measure up on this list. The more you strive, the more honest you are with yourself, the more willing you are to face those hard things you struggle with, the greater of a leader you will become. You know why? Through all that struggle, through all that seeking, through all that change, you will have the necessary grace to help others get through to the other side of their leadership journey. Because you know what it takes to get there by remembering the pain, hard work, and striving of your own journey.

I will indeed tell you, if we are anywhere on the 1-12 list, we are failing miserably and those that we lead have no love for us. For those that do, they will always feel that they personally never measure up, or ever will, to our expectations, praise, or love.

2. Don't Let Your Ego Lead: Look, don't get me wrong, ego can be a good thing! Ego will get you into the room that everyone said you'll never get into. I once had a manager tell me, "You see this key, it's the grand master. This is the key you'll never have. See that office, it's mine. That's the office you'll never have." To which I replied, "I'll have that key and your job in less than a month." You see: Ego. And I did, by the way. Ego can be great!

It can also cause us to make assumptions about what we *think* we know. On the surface, this jobsite was a hard site, full of challenges, Frank was nuts, we had a young staff, our lead foreman never led this many employees on such a large site and the list goes on. These things, though somewhat true, are biased assumptions that ego can latch onto. Assumption clouds our vision and doesn't really allow us to find true root causes.

Once we know that, we can get the job done with

confidence understanding where ego has its place. Also worth noting, strive to never throw around your past experiences to trump others' opinions. Example: I used to work with a young Mining Engineer who would continually remind us about his former work experiences. Anytime that there would be a difference of opinion he would say, "Let me remind you that I am a Mining Engineer", or, " Let me remind you that I have worked for some of the biggest mining companies in the country", and the trifecta, "Allow me to remind you that I am a mining engineer who's worked for some of the biggest Gold mines in the Country, let alone the World." Lord help us! I'll never forget when someone simply replied, "Who gives a shit, bro!"

And that's the rub isn't it? Who gives a shit? Nobody. Not until they realize you give one first. You can have all the education, fame, money, influence, and add whatever else to that list you like. But if you don't show folks you are willing to be humble, not shove your weight around, and that you are striving for real answers, they really don't care what you have to say or what you've done.

I'll never forget watching a program on TV. It was a documentary about life in England and I heard someone say, "I don't give a bullocks! Tell him to come down here and really see what life is like." He was talking about the King of England. The King of all bloody England for heaven's sake! KING! Well, Prince at the time but you get what I am saying. Those rural folks didn't care what the Prince thought. They knew he didn't have a clue as to what they were going through on a daily basis.

There's an old adage that says, "No one cares, until they know *you care*." This goes a long way so before we show up to save the world, make our ego take the back seat for a second so we can really access what is actually going on. In doing so, we will be able to make clear and logical decisions that can work for most folks. Especially if we include them in the process.

3. Don't Make Assumptions: Walking through life I have had a certain set of experiences that has given me the gift of being an empath. I feel what others feel, as if I'm walking in their shoes and I truly hurt for folks who are hurting. And as someone who cares about such things, I strive to find solutions for those in need. Through the process of honing this gift, Anita and I have realized that there is a predictable algorithm to everyday situations, whether they be personal, leadership or otherwise.

The practice of studying commonalities has made me keenly aware of unknown outcomes. I can often see these outcomes way before they happen. On average, when I look at a business, or personal situation, I am right about the outcomes 95% of the time. That's my actual average. My wife and I cannot count all the times I have predicted human behavior to the day, hour, minute, what a person will do. Especially a person who is under pressure. Business after business I have predicted the outcome of a decision they want to make, months before they actually made it. Then I would look like a wizard afterward when it plays out as I had predicted. 95%! I know how arrogant this sounds, but it's true. And being true means only this:

I'M NOT ALWAYS RIGHT, DANG IT!!!!

It's that 5% that makes me realize that if I'm not careful, I will allow my bias to lead the way. Knowing that

I'm not always right, I must, with all intention, dig past what I *think I know* and look for the real answers.

As leaders, we so often assume that we are right. We assume we know the answers before we conduct a true unbiased investigation of the facts. Then, to take it a step further, we take those assumptions and put them under the microscope.

Don't assume anything even if, in the end, you are right. Our job here is to find the actual trends and commonalities to those facts and usher forth an educated conclusion on the present issue. In doing this, you'll find answers and be able to create solid steps to move forward and gain the necessary ground it takes to forge ahead.

This procedure is very much like a **Root Cause Analysis.** With an RCA you are looking deeper than what you see right before your face. Like a tree in front of you is obvious, but when we need to see how it grows, we must look beneath the surface and go to what the roots are feeding on. Though the problems that exist on the surface seem obvious, we must dig deeper and find out what happened before the incident/problem that got us to this point in the first place.

I really like the '5 Whys' by Sakichi Toyoda, the founder of Toyota Industries. The idea in a primitive explanation is to keep asking why until you find the root answer.

Example Incident: I came to work late this morning.
Why: My alarm clock did not go off.
Why: My electricity was shut off.
Why: A tree hit the line.
Why: There was a storm.
Why: High pressure fronts colliding with cold air caused

massive storms in my area causing there to be a lightning strike and a power outage in my neighborhood therefore, causing my alarm clock not to go off.

Now look, That's a really primitive example! But my greater point, whether you are in an office, or, in the field, you can't just jump to conclusions. You owe it to your guys to dig deeper, and find out the root cause of issues, then formulate a plan to get beyond them. The alternative is running into the same issues repeatedly scratching your head wondering 'Why is this still happening?'

4. Don't Give Unreasonable Demands:
"Fix this or you're all going home!" "You have one last shot and if you don't make it happen, you're fired!"
    In the blue-collar world, good leaders are hard to come by. Guys like the tyrant I mentioned above are a dime a dozen. They may start as operators, or dad knew somebody and now they are leading at a less-than-subpar standard. They don't really care, as long as they get paid. And they are never intentional or forward-thinking. You never hear from them or see them out of the office or work truck unless something is wrong. Very seldom are leaders in the field held accountable to a certain set of expectations outside of, 'Exceed production, and don't kill anybody.'
    Throwing ultimatums around, was most assuredly going to add to the stress, bog down the process and not allow our guys to perform at their highest ability. Knowing certain players weren't going anywhere, and I had to work with what I had, and who I had, forced me to

put the demands and threats aside. I had to be a team player, and this made it possible for me to be seen as a guy who was there to help and not to hinder. When we grab hold of this concept, we realize that each team member has their value and can be utilized effectively to launch the team forward. When we don't throw around those ultimatums and throw tantrums, we gain trust; and trust when leading, is everything!

5. Don't Point Fingers: Ownership is everything! As soon as I walked in the door the Lead Foreman started blaming the Site Superintendent, the sites' geological challenges, the weather, or 'The fucking morons HR keeps sending me'. He even threw his leadership team under the bus.

Even though most of these issues were closely true, focusing on them negatively would only breed more strife and contention. There was already enough bitterness on the site. We didn't need more of that. We needed to become lazerbeam focused on the issues at hand and fix them so our guys could keep working. We had heard enough and nipped it right there. Here's what I told our foreman and maybe it will help you when facing these issues.

"Brother, the only person we can blame for our calamity is ourselves. As leaders we are held to a higher standard. We must understand that in order to move forward. If your leadership team isn't supporting you in the way they need to, then you have not communicated properly the way for them to do that. If the site presents challenges, we need to look at what we have in place to consistently combat those challenges. As for Frank, well he's untouchable. Our orders are to get along with him at all costs. So, even though I want to tell him to 'fuck off' just as bad as you do, that cannot be the basis of our focus. All we can do is take one intentional step at a time to move forward, own our shit and I am here to help you do just that. I won't leave you unsupported."

I had this very same conversation with all of the leaders, then eventually all the employees there. After that, there were no excuses. The standard was set. Accountability to that standard was held. My friends, if we are the kind of person or leader who can't stand up and own our mistakes, then we have no integrity. That's all there is to it. Pointing fingers will only delegitimize our word to those we lead and follow. When we step into the role of leader, 'the devil made me do it' mentality has to be thrown right out the window if we're ever to be respected by our subordinates, or those in the chain of command above us.

Every time we pass the buck in our lives is the very moment we give a foothold to mediocrity and diminishes our honor just a little bit more. This kind of living gives way to bigger compromises when you don't decide to stand your ground and take ownership over your involvement in any given situation.

I know it can be hard, and we often put it off till next time. But when we do this, we make a practice of doing so and set a precedent for the rest of our lives. One day that precedent will come to call. And it won't be pretty. I'm living proof.

What I am proud to say, and I feel must be mentioned here is that while sitting in this foreman's office several days later, the phone rang, and it was our exec team. Sitting behind his desk, reluctantly he answered, then to my surprise put the phone on speaker. The exec team was asking all sorts of probing questions, ready to be reactive as always. I could not believe what I heard our lead Forman say: "Hey, this is how it is. This site has gotten out of my grasp. I was too afraid to ask for help. It's so big with so many moving parts. It is my inexperience and I take complete ownership over the state of things and will do my utmost to rectify this. With Mikel's help, and the help of my team I know we can and will turn things around."

OWNERSHIP! PROUD OF YA BROTHER!

6. Don't Focus On The Negatives or Bemoan Your Station: Though the negatives were there to smack me right in the face, I did not allow them to weigh me down. Strive to make sure to have a support system in place during difficult moments like this one. For me it was my wife, my friend Levi, and the professionals, to share the day-to-day issues I faced. Strive also to not be negative around those you lead. Don't bring them down! Encourage them and while you together are fighting the issues at hand. I also made sure to support Frank. Look now, like I've said before, I am not a Saint! I did not like the man and if he got hit by a bus, and I was driving it…. ok just kidding. I didn't hate the man, but even though he was the way he was, it was my job to serve him, like it or not. So why complain? Why obsess about what we cannot control? So don't give negative responses for negative situations. With everything riding on success of fail, we as a team still needed to be in control of our own actions, not Frank, not the site, or the problems. It is also worth mentioning that, by nature, I am a very negative person. I get bogged down with anger and feeling sorry for myself just like anyone else. I'm not kidding either. I'm terrible with it.

Here's an excerpt from a social media post I wrote not too long ago, mentioning just that very thing:

"I struggle in several places in my life.
Two of those are as follows:
Being overly negative to things I cannot control
And feeling sorry for myself for things I cannot control!
And it is not until I count my many blessings
Walk through life with humble gratitude
It is not until I kick myself in my own ass and stop obsessing
That the view of those two things change
At the end of the day, no one but me is responsible for the following:
1. My attitude
2. My well being
3. The words that come out of my mouth
4. My actions
5. My thoughts
I am the master of my fate and so are you
No matter the circumstance
No matter how others treat you or fail to support you
You and you alone are the only one that can have a fulfilled and happy life!
It's 100% mindset!
Now get out there and crush it this week!
By keeping your mind focused on the things that matter
By not obsessing about what you cannot control
Count your many blessings and stop feeling sorry for yourself and you'll build a legacy that will far surpass your legend and inspire others to do the same!"

This is a paradigm shift in our thinking. When the problems are all in your face it's easy to get overwhelmed. But I will tell you this, when we do nothing but share those negative vibes with those we lead, when we do nothing but slam the execs and higher ups, we bring down the whole team. Production dies, safety goes right out the window, and our people suffer. We must be solutions-focused! I'm getting ahead of myself here but if we allow ourselves to sit back and take a breather, then cognitively reset, the we can clearly see the next right thing to do. Especially if you are an over-thinker, like me.

Step back, clear your mind, and prioritize the next right thing to do. Not *all* the next right things. The next right thing. Prioritize then execute. When you realize that negative thinking equals negative results, you will strive to find ways to look at the positives and move forward.

7. Don't Pump Your People Full Of Placebos:

(plə-'sē-bō), plural placebos: **usually a pharmacologically inert preparation prescribed more for the mental relief of the patient than for its actual effect on a disorder.**: an inert or innocuous substance used especially in controlled experiments testing the efficacy of another substance (as a drug) (webster online dictionary)

We've all been there. Culture is crumbling, the heavy season for your industry comes, and everybody is stressed out. Errors become prevalent, morale is low, and the back channels of the organization are on fire with complaints. Then, here comes the manager, the president, or the foreman with the proverbial "Culture Day" or "Let's take the guys out for dinner", as if one or two days of ego stroking and narrative bending, along with a steak and a beer will make all your problems go away. And they do, for a week or two, or at least they seem to until the dopamine-dump wears off. Once the feel-good is gone, the organizational problems still exist. This kind of problem solving is like putting a sheet over the elephant in the room. Oh, it's still there, mind you, but you can't technically see it. We at Bowman Legacies call this 'Dopamine Culture' and we see it happening in every kind of industry our clients work in, ranging from advertising to mining.

Another place we see this happening is in the behavioral portion of our consulting. Not only do we consult on Leadership Development and Organizational Culture, but we also focus heavily on the individual with our one-on-one Personal Development side. And this kind of behavior is killing relationships and businesses as long as there has been a human race! Narcissism is at the very helm of this issue, and it has infiltrated every aspect of our modern way of life. From Myspace to Facebook, Twitter, Instagram, and whatever else will come next, the World has become a very small place. And at the very center of those platforms is the idea that the World needs to see your cat. What I mean is, it's all about 'me, baby', and the World needs to see how great me, myself, and I is.

Unfortunately, these platforms exacerbate and expound a huge problem that leaks into the way we live life, and the way we do business.

Let's look at how many narcissists attempt to fix a problem. When a narcissist wants to fix a problem and a fire rises in a relationship or business, they are quick to offer resolution. This resolution is typically hollow and superficial at its core. Gift-giving, for instance, can be used as a quick token to make it all go away. "Cheers and beers will fix the problem." .... NO. IT WON'T! I'm not saying I didn't take my people out to eat. Yes, I fed them and fed them often, but it was intentional and it wasn't about getting them drunk. It was about getting them away from the jobsite, so I could get inside their heads. It was paramount to hear what they had to say, uninterrupted, unflinching. It was time to be on a fact-finding mission, not a vacation on the company's dime.

When the gift-giving doesn't seem to work, the narcissist will fall apart. This form of resolution doesn't work because he's trying to put a Band-Aid over a gaping wound. He will then shift gears and say that you are the problem. Instead of looking within, and taking ownership, he turns on you, simply because he is unable to see himself as the villain in any scenario. This causes the other person in the relationship, or employee to feel as though they are going crazy. They will begin to ask themselves things like, "Am I really the problem?" "Am I crazy here?" Leading this way makes for a really corrosive place to work. The reason for this is because the narcissist is very convincing and typically a phenomenal wordsmith. He is good at convincing you that the knife he is sticking in you is good for you. Narcissistic leaders can turn a conversation around in a split second because they have lived a lifetime of dodging responsibility and truth in order to come out on top every time. So, what started out as an opportunity to own their mistakes, and really take some positive ground, now becomes a dog fight.

He should be looking for ways where he can change, and for a real resolution to the issues you face together in the relationship. Instead, he will gain followers/allies to his cause in order to weed you out and triumph over you, as if you are now considered the enemy. Everything, I mean every problem is now your fault and he will do all he can to mar your name or remove you from his life because even the sight of you indicates that he is somehow flawed.

It's the same way in business. Instead of looking operationally, instead of looking at what execs are doing, instead of looking inwardly, the view becomes all about weeding out those who do not fit culturally. And now, because the cheers and beers didn't fix the problem, a witch-hunt begins to get rid of all those who are unfaithful. Because obviously we chose the wrong people. When Dopamine Culture fails to work, a whole new negative culture is born. This is when a business transfers to what we at Bowman Legacies call, Narcissistic Culture, and if it persists it becomes something even more elusive and dangerous: Cult Culture.

We have all seen this happen so many times in the industries we have worked. And for those that want to lead from the middle or lead at all, this kind of culture must be an unacceptable approach. We cannot afford to go down the rabbit hole of pats on the back and baby kissing and ignoring the real issues. Because we know all too well how that will fail to work. WE also know what it will cost us in the long run. It's just not worth it.

For me, I had a limited time to fix a very big problem. Though I could not face-down a budding Cult Culture alone, I could lead from the middle and at the very least bring order and a sense of teamwork to our site. You can too!

Honestly, not schmoozing our guys and not trying to suck up to them right away gave me great street cred with our field staff. Trust me reader, they are used to the game. "Oh, they'll come over here and take us out, thinking that fixes everything." (I've heard those very words in the job trailer.) And to be honest, I have taken that very same approach thinking it would work. So, before you start politicking and throwing that money around with dinners and booze, look first to the real issues at hand. It took me a while to learn that the only thing that fixes problems is real integral ownership, intentional plans forward, and execution of said plan. Then take data and try again with the new knowledge. Rinse, and repeat.

8. Don't Be In a Hurry: Too many leaders want to show up, blow up, and blow out. If they can't put a Band-Aid on the issue, they get cross. And who can blame them? Especially when they have so many other irons in the fire. The quick fix is the go-to with most things and when there's a deeper cultural issue going on, it takes a person who is passionate about leadership to see the issues and strive to mend them. Many leaders in business today are set up for failure at jump street. Companies fail to support their people beginning at onboarding and unfortunately it doesn't get better as time progresses. That's right, the moment they walked through the door there was already enough on their shoulders that they have no choice but to sink or swim. The company furthermore compounds the issue by wanting quick resolutions to difficult problems. Because now, the organization is in such peril culturally and operationally, that they are constantly hiring a new savior. Nine times out of ten, in less than a year that guy is on the cross and they are looking for someone else. We get smacked in the face with the problem, and everyone's opinion on why the problem exists, that it can cause us to make rash decisions/assumptions. Combine that with the pressure to get that next homerun put on you by management, and you're dealing with one heck of a stressful situation, with no hope of resolving it. All of that was true in my case as well.

I had a lot of other responsibilities for the organization I worked for. This job site was not the only thing I had going on. Fortunately, for me, I had enough support from other team members that it was possible to shift my responsibilities temporarily, and could almost solely focus on getting this site back on track. Not everyone has that luxury. In this way I was very lucky.

With the ability to take my time, slow down, and focus on the issue at hand, the resolution came.

I had to put out of my mind all the rash statements, all the unrealistic prods to "just fix it," and put my energy and efforts into getting data. Real, honest data was needed. And in order to get that real data I needed real time. This problem didn't happen overnight. Neither did yours so slow down, take it one issue at a time, and don't go it alone. Draw your team in and utilize their strengths.

So as hard as it was to be away from my family, when I love them more than anything in the world, I realized that I needed to sit back and settle in. This kind of approach takes all that panic and anxiety out of your issue and causes you to be able to think clearly and execute decisively.

9
WHAT I DID DO

It can be a very easy thing to harbor bitterness toward someone or something when consistently it has caused you grief. No matter what, even with all this stacked against us, we cannot allow bitterness to creep in and cause us to fail. Remember what not to do is half the battle. What *to do* is the other half of the battle. What we have to realize is, everything we don't have a clue about will come out in the wash as long as we strive to keep balance. Following is a list of what I did do.

1. **<u>We must have an insatiable desire to see everyone in the room win!</u>** This is my number one rule for every leader. This must be at the heart of every action you take. If you don't have an insatiable desire to see everyone in the room to win, you are making a huge mistake! If you don't have an insatiable desire for everyone in the room to win, that means you are in this for the wrong reasons.

If you don't have this desire, it shows clearly that you don't understand servant leadership and you are not an at-all-cost-winner. That's harsh. I realize that. For me however, I have learned the more we serve, the more we carry the sword and shield of our endeavor or the endeavor of others, the more we care about those with us on the field of battle, the more consistently we win! After all I had been through with this business, with this site, with its leaders, I still wanted everyone in the room to win even if I didn't like them.

I wanted:

FRANK TO WIN ~ How can I help Frank win?

OUR LEADERS TO WIN ~ How can I help our Leaders win?

OUR WORKERS TO WIN ~ How can I help our Workers win?

OUR CUSTOMER TO WIN ~ How can I help our customer win?

FOR MYSELF TO WIN! ~ How can I win?

When I broke down our site's issues in this way. I could formulate a plan for each individual area and strive to execute that plan accordingly. That's right, I even had a plan for Frank to win! Ha! Please understand my heart. We don't have to like the guy, the circumstance, the company, to serve them well and want to see them win. Even if the company we work for mistreats us, we should never steal even so much as time from them. We must no longer care about the promises they made us; We must with all intention care about the one we made them when we hired on. Remember, you said you would serve when you signed on. You said you would give it your all. Hell or high water you must be the one to strive to make that happen. Not because they pay you, but because that is what you promised you would do. Striving to see everyone in the room win, and doing our part to make it happen has been a very winning combination in my life. Therefore, having the need to serve in this manner I have won a lot! I've lost some too but when I did, I owned it, learned from it, and rose above it. I also kept my integrity and slept well knowing that I gave it my all and so will you. For me, if I am involved in a process, I desperately want to serve my post and be a part of the answers. When I realize that I am part of the problem it bothers me greatly.

After you realize this, consider not going it alone by drawing others you work with into moving ahead together and maybe your list will look more like this.

We want:

FRANK TO WIN ~ How can we help Frank win?

OUR LEADERS TO WIN ~ How can we help our Leaders win?

OUR WORKERS TO WIN ~ How can we help our Workers win?

OUR CUSTOMER TO WIN ~ How can we help our customer win?

FOR MYSELF TO WIN! ~ How can we win?

Ok, so maybe that's not your schtick. Look at it this way. If things aren't going well in your business/marriage/life and you are about to lose everything, what wouldn't you change to make the necessary adjustments to win? I asked a business leader this question once and he told me flat out he would stop at nothing to make his organization win. When I told him that he needed to change and serve on a higher level he took that challenge head on and I watched him win. He's still winning as a matter of fact. As my longest client I've seen this guy win year after year. Why? One concept. He has an insatiable desire to see everyone in the room win! And when you have this desire, when you build this up within you, you usher hope in the hearts of those you lead. When you do that, you put a spark for the flame that is necessary for you to win as well.

2. You Must Listen! We need to listen to our client on the issues at hand. We need to listen to our employees about the current problems. We need to listen to our employees about their hopes for more in the company and their careers. We need to listen to their stories of home/family/hopes/dreams. We need to listen to the site. Yes, the site.
I drove around a lot. I monitored the weather, I watched the yard, the ready line, the pit, the haul roads, the job trailer. I even befriended a raven for heaven's sake! I wanted to see how that place lived and breathed in every moving part in

order to be able to make decisions in real time that actually made a difference for all aspects of the job.

3. Include Them In The Process: Including our guys in the decision making process, leaning on their wisdom, while holding them accountable to execute was a real game changer.

Most of the time when a 'fixer' or a consultant comes down from on high, there's a lot of telling folks what to do. Leaders get so bogged down in what they think they know it's hard for them to learn anything new. That was ok for us when we were 20. Not when we are in a leadership position. One must realize that you don't know everything. Involve your people into the process. We had a guy on our crew that everyone called grandpa. 'Grandpa' was an older Kentuckian that came from coal. He has moved dirt his entire life. He was also one of the most mellow guys I've ever met in the mining industry. He didn't get bent out of round about a darn thing. This dude knew more about mining than anybody on that site! Now allow yourself to look deeper. Find those "Grandpas!" Together, you can capitalize on so much knowledge you didn't have. Knowledge like:

~What's going on behind the curtain.

~What's going on in the field.

~How the staffers live, breath, and what they are saying.

~Years of life, and craft knowledge on how to fix the current issue.

You see, by including your guys in the process, you are really gaining a tone of knowledge and viewpoints you may have never considered. As we draw in our current leaders and engage them into the process of fixing the current issues, it gives them ownership in seeing the positive changes as they execute the plan you all have created.

This without a doubt is one of the most powerful gifts I can give you. My friends, we are in one of the most fatherless worlds our human existence has ever seen. So many of the employees coming in and out of your organization only need to be guided with a genuinely intentional hand toward victory. All they need is someone to step up and say, "I see greatness in you and I want to help you attain victory." Add bringing them into the process and empowering them to fix issues from the ground up and you will build a team so powerful, so overwhelmingly nimble, and quick to change that you will roll over any obstacle that gets in your way.

Please listen to this friend! Once you have real data, not the skewed view of disgruntled employees, but real honest data on what the problem is, it's time to bring those involved to the table and come to a resolution. Everyone at that table must take 100% ownership. Everyone at that table needs to make 100% amends. Everyone at that table needs to be 100% vested in making this right and forging ahead.

And when the problems go away, or at least subside and you have them on the run. This is the time for cheers and beers! This is the time to celebrate their progress and allow everyone to know who was involved and how many heads they took in the battle. This is the time you sing their praises and let the powers that be know who the heroes are!

Linking shields as a team is no joke! It's about putting self aside and doing what's better for the team. It's about looking at everything including your own actions with such acceptance for the naked truth that you are willing to forge ahead no matter the cost. Linking shields is about having the integrity to be there even for the employee that you don't like in order to get the job done.

This kind of life is not for the timid or weak of mind, thought and deed. It's bigger than anyone ever anticipated, costs more of you, and in the end, will have a higher value than anything you've ever endeavored to do in the workplace.

This way of leading, caused my team to want to work harder to keep things going knowing they were an integral part of the process. This filled them with the pride of knowing that they were part of the process of moving forward and not just being part of the problem. This gave them hope!

4. **Tackle One Problem At A Time:** When we look at the whole picture it is easy to get overwhelmed especially when the problem seems so big. There we are with a huge list of problems; being told we need to change it right away. Fighting on all those different fronts is unstrategic. At first, we have all the energy in the whole world, and it goes well for a while. But after some time, with issue after issue persisting, we as leaders get worn out and burn out entirely and the rapid decline in our want-to begins.

What we must first understand is a simple principle. That principle is this, we are building our lives, and jobs for longevity. When facing this issue, or any other, we tend to get overwhelmed. Maybe that's just me. And what we need to remind ourselves of is this. If we can find out what the most pertinent issue or threat we face is, and execute a plan to resolve it, then we are one step closer to resolving the whole issue.

Worth noting, when we tackle the biggest of many issues, your whole day goes easier once it's resolved. All the other problems seem simpler to fix. For me more than anything, the biggest problem we faced was the whole team hated each other! Once that was resolved a lot of other problems just took care of themselves. It's amazing what can happen when the team's emotional issues have been resolved. Once everyone is on the same team again, a lot of the small issues run more smoothly and don't even need to be mentioned. The second problem now has the attention of the team as a whole and it's not just you hammering away at it.

So next time you get in a jam, and the boss says, 'GO FIX IT!' don't allow yourself to get overwhelmed. Find out all the data, get people on the same page, find out the most pertinent issue, formulate a plan with your team accordingly, and execute that plan.

After you resolve that first problem, recognize those who were pertinent in the victory, celebrate their efforts, and move to the next. In doing so my friend you will find out that you will get less stressed out and have more wind in your sails to move on to new challenges.

5. Get In The Dirt With Them: 'Get in the Dirt' with your People! Whatever that looks like for your industry! I cannot count how many late nights, muddy steel-toed boots, and busted knuckles I have had coming home to my hotel. I still feel bad for the cleaning ladies as I tried, I really did, but no matter how careful I was, the next morning sure enough there was mud dried somewhere on the carpet. My wife would stop me on the porch many times. "Hold it! Strip em right there and I'll throw them in the wash!" I don't blame her either. I was covered on more than one occasion with hydraulic fluid, hammer oil, and grease. Even as a safety man I was more than willing to jump into equipment or help turn a wrench.

At our California site things were no different. I rode around in haul trucks, took out the trash, cleaned the work trailer bathroom (Lord there's a crown in Heaven waiting for that one), and whatever else was needed. I'm still that way. And you know why? Knowing full well what it is like to be covered in filth, busting my ass and looking up to see someone just standing there. Either an exec, or a fellow worker watching you struggle when they know full well things could go a lot quicker if they would just lend a hand. When you decide you are above doing certain things, your team feels it. They see that you will ask them to do things that you yourself would never even attempt. When you put this kind of separation in your team, you will never gain their trust and respect.

There's a book called **Men Against the Sea,** written by Charles Nordoff and James Norman Hall. It is a story of a Captain Bligh and the mutiny of his ship The Bounty. You should really read this book if you aspire to lead. This is a great example of *what not to do* as a leader, and how to turn it around in the most horrible of circumstances.

At one point the men in the book had been kicked off the ship The Bounty and were out to sea on a small lifeboat. In their many adventures during this time covering almost 1100 nautical miles, they were preparing to anchor near an island hoping to find food and fresh water. For five nautical miles a huge shark the length of the boat followed them. The closer they got to land they noticed an enormous crocodile swim under the boat. (This is a true story, by the way.)

Bligh gave the orders to drop the anchor and when said anchor tightened the slack of the rope to which it was attached, the rope broke! Down went their anchor in shark/crocodile infested waters. Ok, now if I were half-starved, being chased by natives who were trying to eat me, out to sea in a small boat with no firearms to protect me with 18 others, as soon as that damn rope broke, you know what I would be thinking? "Don't pick me, please, oh please don't pick me to get that anchor!"

But before the men could even ask who the poor soul would be to have to do it, they heard a *splash*! And sure enough, their Captain went overboard, head over heels to do the dirty work! When he surfaced and all was done, one of the sailors thanked him for his heroic act, then asked why the captain didn't just pick one of the others to do this horrible task. To this he said something to the effect of, "I had that shark on my mind the entire time. And what was it that we saw? Oh yes, a crocodile! I would not ask of my men what I myself would not do."

This my friends, is Getting in the dirt!
Or in his case: Getting in the water!

6. Fill Your Men with Fire! Fill your team with hope! Day after day, our people forge ahead into the workplace only to be led by managers, Forman, and superintendents, who are about as effective as a wet rag, instead of an inspirational leader. They drag themselves in, first thing in the morning, coffee in hand, give a half ass meeting, half ass toolbox talk, half ass game plan, then plod off into their office like a barn-sour horse. Enough is enough! You fail to see the possible impact you have on the people you lead, and it shows!

IT SHOWS IN PRODUCTION!

IT SHOWS IN YOUR SAFETY RECORD!

IT SHOWS IN EMPLOYEE ENGAGEMENT!

IT SHOWS IN RECRUITING!

IT SHOWS IN RETENTION!

As leaders, if we will allow ourselves to see how tremendously successful we can be when we decide that Leading from the Middle, is what prepares us for Leading from the Top. If we can see that this life we lead is so much bigger than what we see at the end of our noses and there's a whole world of people just waiting to be led and mentored, we will begin to draw to us an unstoppable team. In this moment is when the light comes on in your head. If you strive to help others on your team be successful, then you will also be successful. We will turn the dirt world, and maybe even the corporate world around!

We must get in our heads that life, and work, is so much BIGGER THAN YOU! If you are in a place of Leadership, YOU have the Opportunity to Lead on a High Level and ETERNALLY CHANGE the Lives of your Workers, your Families, and your Friends! Your Life CAN make a difference, CAN mean more! If you could Strive to see the GREATNESS IN YOURSELF, and those whom you share life with, and Strive to help others achieve GREAT things, then YOU can Build such a Legacy that it will never EVER be Forgotten!!

It is Time our people learn lessons from us BIGGER THAN:

WHAT NOT TO DO

WHO NOT TO BE

WHAT NOT TO SAY

HOW NOT TO TREAT PEOPLE!

There your people stand awaiting your orders first thing in the morning, or that late night meeting. They are learning from you. Gleaning from your bad mood, your lack of passion, your passive aggressive attitude, your inconsistent leadership and guidance. Every move you make as a leader, whether you are a President, CEO, or leading somewhere from the middle is being watched, learned from, gleaned from, emulated, acted out and you wonder why your team, or organizations' culture is flat as a pancake? You don't have to be the Tony Robbins of the office. But for Pete's sake realize the influence you have on your team can be leveraged for good or bad.

I'll never forget peering over a berm observing our crew go down tricky switchbacks to load out material. Attempting to encourage our leader at the site I said, "You've got a good crew, brother. You must only guide them toward success. Fill them with fire, fill them with hope. Invest even in the least of them and you'll have men that will follow you to hell and back. We've turned this site around in two and a half weeks, now keep the momentum going! I believe in you! I've forged the path for you, now walk it!" Slowly the foreman turned his head and looked at me and his words haunt me still today. "Mikel, I'm not you. I can't inspire people like you do. And to tell you the truth even if I could, I dare say I wouldn't. I don't really like people. For the most part I hate them and couldn't care less what happens to any of these guys. I mean I don't wish harm on any of them of course. But fact is, I only care what happens to me." Reader, if only you were there. This was said to me in the coldest, deadest tone a human could muster. This was this guy's truth, the narrative that he walked around with in life, and he wondered why he was failing like hell-wouldn't-have it.

7. Let them Hold You Accountable: I allowed even the most entry level guy we had hold me accountable to the rules and expectations set forward for the team. This is where most leaders and companies fail. They walk around with the "I'm the boss and what I say goes" mentality. Corrosive leaders hold their people accountable to ideals and rules that they themselves would never submit too. This kind of separation of class, so to speak, is the very thing that has caused the recruiting and retention problem in this country. For far too long leaders of sites, offices, or companies have stood on the necks of those they lead in such an oppressive way that no one wants to work in the blue-collar world anymore. Why should they give so much of themselves, why should they spend more time at work than at home? Why put up with corrosive leadership who are following the same old template? Especially when a lot of dads are telling their kids, "Don't do this son! You should find a job that doesn't take up so much of your life. Money isn't everything."

When you allow even the most entry level employee or team member to hold you accountable, you give them ownership over the culture. You also give them a say and an influence over the cultural environment they are in. This is so powerful, when most places are telling them they are at the mercy of whatever madness the execs roll out. When you do not allow your team to hold you accountable to the same rules, you are no different than everyone else, and it is a dangerous place for a team/organization. We want to be a solid place to work, who looks out for their own. When the word gets out that you are just like everyone else, no matter what your Instagram or website looks like, recruiting will be a nightmare! Once the word is out, it's very difficult to turn that kind of cultural blunder around.

Now you might be thinking, "Mikel, who cares? It's just a job, right? They hire you to do X and you do X and they pay you. Why invest? Why allow employees to keep you accountable to ideals or expectations you have for them? This is how the World works!".This is how the world works…Umm… and you realize the world is fucked up right? Give me just a little more of your time and I will map out more of my methodology, and continue to show you the results in doing it differently than the rest of the world.

8. Recognized & Utilized Talent: There was no way I was going to accomplish this goal on my own. I did not possess enough mining knowledge to make all the right decisions so to say that the success of this site was going to rest solely on my shoulders is a ridiculous notion. So recognize talent and utilize those people irregardless if you are best buddies. Stop promoting your brother-in-law if he sucks at his job. Promote, and praise those that have the talent and the want to.

We had a day shift supervisor who led the whole operation. He had two lead foreman on dayshift. He also had a night lead foreman, who had two guys he called foreman to help him. Working in more than one area of the mine site meant our guys needed to have solid supervision and what I realized is that we had all the talent we needed. We just needed to help them play to their strengths.

One of our leaders on the night shift was really good with the guys. Danny was charismatic and well liked amongst the men. He was also a very talented operator. Putting him over nights made it easier for us to lead and inspire him to take a bigger role in getting our guys working together. All he needed was a small nudge and a little mentoring. Where he lacked was accountability, which is common amongst most young leaders. When I was young, I wanted to inspire others, I wanted to lead, but I also wanted people to like me. Those two things don't always coincide well.

On day shift we had a couple of Marine Corps Vets who knew how to keep the guys on task. But no one had given them any authority. It was a no-brainer that this needed to change! One particular fellow from Indianapolis, Indiana really showed potential. He was tall, well spoken and motivated. One afternoon, a supervisor didn't perform a toolbox talk, so he jumped in there and did it! It came naturally, and he showed me one of his strengths that day, and I was so pleased he did. Pulling him aside, I explained to him from that moment on, not to hesitate to give his opinion and speak up.

A supervisor had previously told him that he was a pain in the ass. This particular worker, also mentioned he didn't think he should rock the boat because he was black. I told him "Rock the damn boat, baby! Especially when it's sinking like this one is! We need all the people we can get bailing water and you have leader written all over you! Get out there and lead! And if you need reigned back in, I'll do so! And, if you need me to get your back, you have it!" I said these things in front of the crew, so when this man spoke up, they knew to listen.

Earlier I mentioned a guy a lot of folks called grandpa. Some of us called him the old dog. Grandpa had been around in the mining world for so long, his years of experience was a huge value to me and the team. So, I went to him often for advice. He didn't get wound up about much at all. Grandpa had a talent for taking some of our more rowdy boys under his wing and I was purposeful about pointing out the ones that could use a little guidance. I dare say with guys like Grandpa you can accomplished unimaginable things!

You see, take the guys that you know have talent and use it to your advantage. Noticing what they were good at and playing to their strengths. That's not manipulation, that's Leadership! Sometimes the answer isn't to hire more workers. Look around and see what/who you have right in front of you and challenge them to rise up. Deep down, we all perform better when we are challenged. Give your team the opportunity to do so. Statistics tell us that people are leaving their jobs because they don't have the opportunity to grow; they aren't challenged! So, with the recruiting issues our country is facing now, let's get more focused on the talent we have on our teams and retaining that talent!

Let's break it all down into a checklist to measure your performance :

What Not to Do

1. **Don't yell, threaten or belittle people.** This only makes matters and performance worse. Besides, all the yelling in the world won't fix most problems and you only end up coming across like a broodish child who is inept at leading others.
2. **Don't let your ego lead:** Put your ego aside and learn to become a servant leader. In the long run people will respect you more and go further with you.
3. **Don't make assumptions:** Yes, the issues may be glaringly blatant. They might be right in front of you. But put away what you think you know and dig for the facts of what the root problems actually are.
4. **Don't give unreasonable demands:** This is where fatalities, and accidents happen. When you give those unreasonable demands and people fight to meet them, things get forgotten, misplaced, unchecked.
5. **Don't point fingers:** When problems are this bad, you don't have time for the he said/she said game. It's time to take ownership as a whole, and move forward as a whole. You can get to the bottom of whodunnit later. The client needs to see action, they need to be reassured you have things well at hand.
6. **Don't focus on negativity and stay positive:** A forward thinking and moving leader puts the pity party aside and keeps their head in the game. Now is the time for keeping yourself focused on what you

have to do to win and keeping your team reassured you can and will win.
7. **<u>Don't Give Out Placebos:</u>** As you grow as a leader, more and more begin to see how corrosive the "safety incentive plans," the "Take em out for dinner, that will fix everything," the "inspirational phone chat from the president," truly are. With no real change behind these gestures, you are only delaying the inevitable.
8. **<u>Don't be in a hurry:</u>** Slow down! Let nothing or no one spin you into a panic. You are a leader. You are the one responsible. Take one issue at a time and crush it, obliterate it, and move to the next one. Rush, rush, rush, only makes matters worse. It's like being in a hurry trying to untie a knotted string. You will only make the knot worse.

<u>What To Do:</u>

1. **<u>Have an insatiable desire to see everyone in the room win:</u>** Yup, even the guy you don't like. When you are Leading from the Middle, and you realize in order for you to win, everyone else needs to win. Wanting everyone to win isn't enough. You have to make choices and act in such a way that backs up that realization.

2. **<u>Truly Listen:</u>** I heard it once said, "Mikel, folks typically won't listen, until they know you are willing to first." If you want to gain trust and loyalty, it

begins here. Listen, learn, and be slow to speak. Ask lots of questions, and gain knowledge like Sherlock Holmes.

3. **Include Your Team In The Decision Making Process:** Too many execs do just the opposite. Don't be that guy! Include your people in the decision-making process, get them involved and they will have pride and ownership of the outcome.

4. **Tackle One Problem At a Time:** I know this may sound impossible especially in multifaceted sites. Gather all the data, get people on the same page, Define the most pertinent issue, formulate a plan with your team accordingly, and execute that plan.

5. Once you are able to prioritize and execute, man that made all the difference in the world!

6. **Get In the Dirt With Your People:** As a safety guy I ran equipment, helped maintenance, troubleshoot, and replace hydraulic lines. As an exec, I cleaned out tracks, took out the trash, cleaned toilets, talked to my people at 3a.m. Get in the mud and the muck, Show them you are willing to do anything they are doing to get the job done. Show them you care and are a part of the team. Show them by your example and you can't imagine how much your people will respect you for it.

7. **Fill Your People With Fire!** There's nothing worse than a wet blanket, doom and gloom leader! If you lack charisma, you will be putting your team and your production goals to sleep! Wake up! Get excited! Fill your people with hope! Be the kind of

leader that inspires your people to move just a little bit farther, harder, higher.

8. **Allow Them To Hold You Accountable:** At Bowman Legacies we have built something called the Problem Protocol. This is an S.O.P. for communication and problem solving. One of the rules demands you don't complain, but instead, look for answers!

    I came into the house one day really angry, talking about our insane neighbors. My youngest daughter looked up at me and said, "Poppa, sounds like to me you are just complaining. The Problem Protocol which you created says not to complain." Dang it! She had me dead to rights. She held me accountable, and you need to let your team do the same for you without you getting butt hurt about it.

9. **Recognize And Utilize Talent:** Play to your team's strengths. Truly give a hard look at each individual member of your team and ask the question: Where do they strive? What are they best at? How can I help them thrive?

Fact is when we approach leadership like we know it all, can do it all, we come across like a dick! Fact! We need to engage the people we have and play to their strengths. When my boss came several weeks later, he said he could not believe the change in the site. Even Frank was happy. I did not do that alone. No leader worth his salt ever does.

Every guy on that site that worked for us deserves a medal for how hard they all tried to turn things around.

10
A LINE IN THE SAND

Please allow me to share where leading from the middle started for me. Many years before we started Bowman Legacies, many years before the job in California, for which this book is mostly about, I worked in the non-for-profit space. We were living in Florida, struggling with living life, and my feeling was my life was going nowhere fast. At the time was working as a maintenance man at a church that boasted fifteen thousand members. The culture was so poor, the morale so bad, the leadership so arrogant, it made for a very difficult place to work. Up to that point in my life, my greatest hope was to be a pastor. A dream that had lingered for many years, however seeing how this place ran the dream began to die.

I had enough of the job's cultural issues allowing them to make me sour and hate my life. Unfortunately, I allowed other people's poor attitudes to affect mine in such a way that I was not a good employee. More and more the realization came to me that my attitude alone had much to do with me getting miserable at work. Not dealing with my bad attitude, combined with unresolved childhood trauma, I had a nervous breakdown and quit my job. Bad thing was, I was married and we had a newborn baby. I just couldn't take it a day longer! Looking back, I don't regret leaving that soulless place, one bit. Volumes of books could be written about what not to do from my years working in that church. I may write about it one day.

At any rate, I left there and found a job at a local university as a maintenance man. Rumor was that you could get an enormous discount on classes as a full-time employee. For me it was a game changer in more ways than I ever could imagine, but this time had to be different. I could not allow myself to get so jaded and miserable at yet another job. Knowing right off the get-go that my own attitude had to be reigned in and had to prove to myself it could be done. Every job has its ups and downs, but back in those days the downs kept me down. I felt with the classes being discounted there was a great opportunity to move ahead, and I didn't want to mess it up by allowing poor attitudes to ruin my thinking. It would also be inevitable that at some point I would befriend someone on staff, and that person would fill me in on all the drama and dissension at work. It was time to be prepared and not to allow the bad parts of the job to jade me. I had to be prepared to make up my own mind and keep a good attitude in order to leverage this new opportunity.

Sure enough, day one I got the rundown. My new boss had, for the most part, given me zero information on what my job entailed. I didn't even know where to clock-in let alone what my responsibilities were. My new boss had a fellow we'll call Dan to show me the ropes. He was a tall handsome young man, who was eager to show me around and get me up to speed on what was what. As soon as we left the bosses office, Dan began to fill me in. "Ok here goes, I can already tell you are going to get along just fine with the young guys around here. Fact is Mikel, it's the old guys against the young guys in this place. On one side the old guys stick to themselves, claiming we never clean up after ourselves or bring back their tools. (After being there a week that proved to be true). They think all we do is slack off and fool around (also, partially true). Also, seldom if ever ask them for help; they won't show up. If by some chance, they do come to help, all they'll do is boss you around and tell you that you are doing everything wrong." (Completely true).

Dan drove me around for the better part of two hours showing me around the small campus. He pointed out his buildings, took me to all the places he liked to 'hide out', and then took me to my buildings for which I was to be responsible. There at the edge of campus were three run-down buildings that looked more like an abandoned campground than something fit for a university. All three were of block construction and all three needed a new roof, doors, and windows. None of them had bathrooms, and all of them smelled of mold and years of neglect. Two of the buildings were admin offices, and one was an open room building the college used as a classroom, of which, had a porch falling off it!

The other building they gave me was across the road. It was a two-story concrete building that resembled the 'last resort' kind of motel of your nightmares. It consisted of 16 rooms, of which, one was uninhabitable. This gem of a building was called La-Chateau. A sturdy old girl that had all its apartment doors exposed to the elements and the back of the building bordered Lake Bonnie, a crummy little gator-pit at the edge of town.

This my friends explains Lakeland, Florida in the mid-to-late nineties to a capital T. Every little pond, every little drop of water was called a lake. I suppose Lake Bonnie sounded a hell of a lot better than, "Shit, this thing is shallow and full of alligators!" Lake Bonnie seems to have more appeal and makes for a much smaller sign. Much of the town, like this building, was a remnant of another time. Not like the Eiffel Tower, mind you, more like the Titanic. Sunk, moldy, and past fixing. Back in the day when Lakeland, Florida was started, someone decided that 'Mud Pit, Florida' would not sound very good on the visitors flier. So, every retention ditch, and waterway got the word 'lake' slapped at the end of it to make it more palatable to the throng of old people raiding central Florida like a plague of locusts. There they came like an unyielding, golf cart driving, tennis ball on your trailer hitch, golf shorts wearing, fanny pack using, Viking horde! There was money to be made in the world of retirement, and things had to seem and look a certain way to lure that army of retired white folk!

So, Lakeland was born and by the time we and got there, everything was sort of a spooky, shabby-sheek version. Almost as if you combined Glamour Cat and Scooby Doo! La-Chateau was the epitome to a day gone by and a theme to which I had become frighteningly accustomed. As a matter of a fact, this building was so old, and so crummy, so moldy, so god-awful, the students so affectionately called the place 'La-Shithole'. And boy oh boy, did she ever live up to her name! To say the least I had my work cut out for me. Decaying buildings, segmented team, organizationally warring factions, and a whole lot of he said/she said all muddied the waters and made for a poor workplace yet again. That's just something I wasn't willing to stand for. Not this time.

That summer was extremely hot, and as the vengeance of hellish heat came rolling in, our guys were getting grouchier by the minute. To make matters worse, the vice president of the school was very ambitious and had put the needs of the school's remodel above that of the maintenance team's safety. For example, we were not able to wear shorts or lightweight maintenance shirts. Instead, we were required to work in the heat with our heavy thread-count uniforms. With 115-degree heat and 100% heat humidity, and half of our crew beyond retirement age, we needed to take every precaution. Secondly, the request to put a water cooler on every maintenance golf cart was denied, as were requests for sunscreen, and other PPE. Thirdly, (strike three) there was never a meeting and/or process of checking in on one another during the summertime, or during any other inclement weather, for that matter. Mind you, this is Florida where heavy rain, hurricanes and such were a part of our everyday normal. The idea of safety or teamwork was absolutely not part of the work culture here. It was obvious that we were on our own.

I'll never forget Cal. He was an elderly man and if he's still alive today it would only be to the ardent efforts of wizards and shaman. The man shook when he walked like he was doing the boogie-woogie with every step. His frock of snow-white hair was always perfectly parted to one side and his 5'5" figure cast a menacing shadow when he would suddenly appear out of nowhere, which he was accustomed to doing. He was a stickler for detail, unflinching in his duties, a flirt to one of the cafeteria lunch ladies (who turned out to be his wife) and an absolute grouch! I loved Cal for all of these reasons!

However, he made it obvious that us younger guys were not welcome in his portion of the shop. Those were his actual words. "One look at you, and you aren't welcome in my portion of the shop." I was like, well ok. Then he went on. "You youngsters are unruly and dishonest. You never bring my tools back when you borrow them. I don't trust you; I don't like you, and I don't want you here." By the way, those were the first words Cal ever spoke to me, and he said it in the calmest of tones. It was concise and with no malice, he spoke these things, and the rest of the staff his age was of the same sentiment. To strive to bridge the gap I would often ask the older guys to join us at our table for lunch. Everyone took my offer at one time or another; all except for Cal.

There was a day that was so unbearably hot. A guy on my team passed out just as he peaked a two-story ladder, climbing up onto the roof. I just so happened to be standing right there when his eyes roll in the back of his head. I have no idea still to this day how I did it, but with one hand on the ladder, my left foot on the spill ledge of the flat roof, jumped out and grabbed the man by the shirt and brought him in. He stumbled, sweat dripping in his eyes. We made him sit down and got some water and a cold press for his head. Poor guy was drenched. The heat was just too much!

That same day toward the end of my shift I was one of the last to clock out. My buildings were at the other end of the small private campus, and I was delayed that day for one reason or another. While driving up to the shop, I noticed Cal on a park bench leaning to one side. His skin tone was a type of gray, and his shirt was soaked, as were his work pants. The man was slumped and motionless. It didn't take a genius to know what was going on. My heart sank. Up to this point in my life I had seen death many times. And there the old man was, dead as a hammer on a park bench just outside of the tool room he so faithfully managed.

Before getting off the cart I yelled his name, "Cal!" Nothing. I jumped off the cart and ran to him and said his name, "Cal?" Nothing. I sat down on the bench and said his name again. Nothing. I put my hand on his shoulder and that old man jumped like a jack rabbit who had been electrocuted! It scared the ever-loving shit out of me! "Dammit Cal! I thought you were dead!" He didn't even look at me when he got up and walked away. All I got for my concern was, "Why the hell is everybody saying that?!" My heart was pounding so hard you could have used it for the rhythm of a Pantera song! If you've seen the movie Maverick with Mel Gibson, there is a scene where they ask a stage driver if he's feeling alright. Yeah, don't think for a second that wasn't in my mind.

On another occasion, I came into Cal's shop needing a cat's paw, which is a great tool for prying up finish nails, and at the time were kinda hard to come by. We were working and one of the guys said, "Dang, I could use a cat's paw right now." I suggested, "Hey Cal has one in the tool cage. I'll go see if he'll let me borrow it." Everyone stopped what they were doing and looked at me like a monkey just crawled out of my nose. "What?" Someone was quick to answer me, "You'll have to pry that thing out of Cal's dead hands. If he was stroking out on the shop floor, I bet his last words would be, "Bury me with my keys to the tool cage. Oh, and my cat's paw!" Another guy piped up, "If Satan showed up here with a snow cone up his ass, wearing a wool jacket, I might believe it's possible. Don't waste your time, Mikel." I took this as a personal challenge. A cat's paw would make short work of what we were doing, and it would be foolish not to at least ask. Instead of cutting the lock like most of our guys would've done, I went to Cal to ask. "Cal, may I borrow your cat's paw? I know other guys don't bring back your tools, but I'm not the other guys. Not only will I bring it back, but I will replace it with my own money if it gets lost." Cal looked at me with squinted eyes and furrowed brow. "You promise you'll bring it back?" I nodded yes. "And you know what it's used for, right?" I nodded again. "You know that thing is not a spud or a pry bar, right?" I nodded yet again and added, "This is for finishing nails in the paneling for La-Shithole. It will make short and clean work of the job." Reluctantly, Cal plodded over to the tool cage. His keys were attached to a retractable spring-loaded keychain. All the old guys had them. They would pull their keys out, unlock whatever door or cabinet, look dead into your eyes, and let go of the keys, sending them whizzing right back into the nestled spot on their belts, slick as a whistle. When they used them with such bravado, it was like watching James Dean light a cigarette. It would always make me laugh. Cal handed me the cat's paw. I took it and started off, but Cal hadn't let go yet. The old man had a grip like an ape. I jerked to a halt. There we stood, two grown men holding one tool. Just a yard shy from the shop's double doors, I was nearly in the clear but ole' Cal wanted to have one last word before I set off. Cal looked deep into my eyes. He wore bottle cap glasses and his eyes still looked squinty, so I'm guessing here, but I'm pretty sure he was looking into my eyes. "Mikel, if you don't bring this back in the same order it was given, I will never forget it. You keep a sharp eye on it because one of the young guys you work with has sticky fingers, if you know what I mean. I know which one it is and he's had his eye on it, so don't let it out of your sight. You'll not get any help from the likes of me ever again if you don't bring it back." Yeah, no pressure.

Look, let me stop here for a second. Up to this point in my life if a guy had said this to me no matter his age or prowess, I would have told him to piss off! I was really rough around the edges, but this job had to be different, and it had to start with me. I felt that the Lord was asking me to give this guy honor, and every guy for that matter. It was so hard for me to put my pride aside and honor Cal by not cutting the lock off and taking what I wanted. Cal deserved my respect, and I knew he had been ripped off before. "Cal, I know other guys have stolen from you and haven't been honest, but I'll bring it back, or I'll buy you a new one. That's a solemn promise or my name's mud and I deserve whatever wrath you have for me. We square?" Cal smiled and let go. When I returned to La Chateau with the tool, all the guys marveled! I won't mention the vulgar questions of what I had to do to get it, but if you are blue collar enough, I'm sure you can fill in the blanks. The men clapped for me and frankly, it felt like I was finally part of the team. Now all one had to do was make good with my promise to Cal.

The cat's paw made short work of what we were doing and after clean up, and all the scrap taken to the dumpster I looked to the spot where the tool had been laid, of course, it wasn't there. Ole' Mr. Sticky fingers got me, and it wouldn't be the last time either. I looked all over and came up with zero. I went outside to where all the guys were and asked frantically, "Guys! Wait! Anybody seen Cal's cat's paw? I looked all over and I can't find it." Immediately all the guys looked through their cart tool boxes, save one. Oh, he looked, but the lid was barely cracked enough for anyone else to see and his efforts were halfhearted. Worth noting, all the other guys let me look in their cart. Mr. Sticky fingers was off and out of the lot before I could get to his cart. He wheeled off and said, "Try the dumpster where we threw everything away." I did look in the dumpster, guess what, no luck. It was time to call my wife, "Babe, I lost a tool at work and am going to the store to find one and replace it. It's my fault. I'm pretty sure one of the guys stole it but I can't prove it." Off I went to the old guy hardware store. We have one similar to it in Bloomington called Kleindorfer's. I love that place. You know the kind. No lights, no sign, no glamor, smells like oil and fresh cut lumber. Sure enough, they had a cat's paw. It didn't have the wear of a thousand years on it, it wasn't used by Joseph to open the presents of sweet baby Jesus, but it was the best I could do. I thought for sure Cal would roast me for losing his.

Head hung low entering the tool cage I walked lightly, and to my astonishment it was open, wide open. No Cal either. My first instinct was to hang the paw on the hook and run like hell. Maybe the old grouch wouldn't notice. My second thought was, 'Are you kidding, Cal notices when we've moved the lock to one side or another checking if it's latched.' Instead, I shut the cage and was just about to latch the lock when out of the shadows a shaky, "What can I do for you Mr. Bowman?" It wasn't a big room. Where the hell was this guy hiding? "Cal, I don't know how to say this, so here it is. I lost your cat's paw and I have no one to blame but myself. I set it down and went to the dumpster and when I came back it was gone. I looked all over for the damn thing and even jumped in the La-Shithole's dumpster and came up empty. Look, I know this one is different, but I bought it with my own money. I really feel like a heel but…." He cut me short and snatched the tool out of my hand. Cal walked over to the tool cage and hung it in the old ones' spot. Then slowly, intentionally, shut either side of the cage doors and latched the hasp and locked it. "Mikel, I don't care that you lost it. You gave your word. That's good enough for me. I told you old sticky fingers was tricky." He turned and walked toward the back of the shop doors and just before he left, he turned back to me and added. "If you ever need anything again, just let me know."

The next week, guess who joined us at our lunch table? That's right- Cal! Seeing this gave me great joy. I'll never forget the looks on the faces of the other maintenance guys. What was cool on their part was they all greeted Cal with respect and we had a lovely time. I was so proud to see him there sitting with us, and it wouldn't be the last time. Our teams were finally coming together. You see, I gave honor to a grouchy old man who, up to this point, would have nothing to do with anyone else our age on the team. He refused to associate or help them as he had been so jaded by their bad and disrespectful nature. And if it had not been for me wanting to make a change, most likely I would have been very much the same way. You see, I didn't kiss up to Cal, I didn't tell him what he wanted to hear so I could get my way, I didn't ignore him because of his age, I didn't discount his knowledge or feelings, I payed homage to him, I gave him respect first, and it made all the difference.

I learned so much about bringing a team together just from that little interaction with Cal that the decision was made to replicate and perfect it through my entire work career, and it has changed the dynamic of so many companies for the better. Remember this, I wasn't the president of the university. In fact, he was clueless as to what our team needed and the vice president showed his lack of understanding many, many times. I wasn't the maintenance manager. I wasn't even a foreman, or supervisor. I was someone in the MIDDLE trying hard to bring a team together.

On the day I gave my notice that my we were moving back to our home state to be closer to family, my boss said this, "Mikel, your first week here I wanted to fire you until I realized you had food poisoning," (I did too. I lost like 15 pounds) "and besides, Clara wouldn't let me." (It's good to have friends in the executive staff). "Then, I noticed that you were really trying. So I kept you on and I am so glad I did! It's always been the old guys against the new guys and now I have a team. I have you to thank for that! If things don't work out back up north, you have a place here."

This guy wasn't the type of person that beat around the bush or paid compliments where none were warranted. It gave me a feeling of great accomplishment knowing that I had made an impact. You can too! It all starts here. Stop buying into all the negative cultural norms at work and strive to lead with integrity, even if you've just walked through the door. Be the change you want to see and stay consistent in this mission. Not everyone will be on board, but the ones who matter, will. If you stay the course, you will see the change and make the difference you hoped for by Leading from the Middle.

If you go back to the list of the Dos & Don'ts of Leading from the Middle, you'll check a few off here in this situation. Like I said, it all started here. And it was here that I noticed a change in the way I conducted myself and how it affected those on the team around me. You will too, my friend, when you decide to Lead from the Middle. What you will find is that you'll build a strong team of allies, you'll bridge the gap between execs and boots, and more importantly, you'll Build a Legacy that will far Surpass your Legend, while inspiring others to do the same!

11
I'M BOUGHT IN NOW WHAT?

So, you've read this far and you're thinking, 'Mikel I'm on board with what you're saying. I get the fact that I may not be the leader of my organization, I may not even be a foreman, but I know I want to make a difference. So, with that in mind, where do I start?' The concept of Leading from the Middle works whether you are in the executive world, or in the dirt world. And it does not matter where you are in the queue of leadership within the organization you work for, the idea or notion of making a difference for your team and your coworkers is simple. Begin with gaining knowledge. Knowledge is Power. With that in mind, I have some book recommendations that made a major difference for me, in the beginning of my journey. Each of these either taught me something new, or confirmed things thought might be pertinent to leadership. Some of these books you may have read already or may have heard of. Either way, you'll know you're doing the next right thing.

Recommendations are as follows:

1. John C. Maxwell: Failing Forward

2. John C. Maxwell: The 360 Leader

3. John C. Maxwell: The Winning Attitude: Developing the Leaders Around you: Becoming a Person of Influence (Three book titles in one)

4. Jocko Willink & Leif Babin: Extreme Ownership

5. Jocko Willink & Leif Babin: Dichotomy of Leadership

Now, you may shy away from the first three books on the list, if you're not a religious person. However, I have to caution you, do not overlook John C Maxwell's practical knowledge of Leadership. John Maxwell has made an enormous living helping Fortune 500 companies lead on a higher level. So, when you see him do not discount his writings as they are chalked full of great pathways for leading your team and yourself to success.

For those of you who do not know Jocko Willink and Leif Babin, I must say for the budding leader, these two books Extreme Ownership and Dichotomy of Leadership go hand in hand. They will absolutely challenge you in ways you did not expect and is for every leader both new and seasoned.

Extreme Ownership puts the microscope on you personally and teaches you on a micro level how we often defer to passing the buck when problems happen in our own personal lives and organizations. This book powerfully challenges you to take the helm of owning your failures on an extreme level.

Dichotomy of Leadership gives you new tools of understanding how to have that 90-foot view of your team and look way downstream before you ever get started. This book also backs up Extreme Ownership and, in my opinion, they go hand in hand. They are like 2 warriors Linking Shields and are an absolute must for the leader at any level.

Second: What we must understand is that the only enemy we have as a business/team leader is <u>ignorance</u>. Both our ignorance, and the ignorance of those we are trying to lead. I am not saying that we are stupid, by any stretch of the imagination. What I am saying: ignorance is simply what we don't know. And what we don't know can kill us!

This is why knowledge is so vital and as a person wanting to lead on a high level, we must be starving for knowledge, understanding, logic and truth. These skills obtained by gaining knowledge are the guiding light on a darkened path. And often, we are on our own in this, so we must take the helm of guiding our thoughts, hearts, and behaviors in order to influence others so we can win. In order to do that, you need knowledge. As you know, my friend: knowledge is power.

There is an old saying that goes something like this, "Even a fool is considered wise when he is slow to speak." When troubles arise at home, your team, your business, even if you think you know it all, seek knowledge/intel first. Get all the facts, all the commonalities, study them and be slow to make snap judgments. There is another old saying I love, "There is wisdom in a multitude of counselors." Bring that knowledge/data/intel to those who have been there or those you link shields with. As a leader we so often feel we have to be the one to make all the decisions. Not so. Share that knowledge, bring others to the table, and make decisions together even if you are an entry level employee.

Third: I want you to prepare yourself for the feeling of being the only person bailing water on a sinking ship. The endeavor of striving to lead in the middle when you are not the CEO or the president, can often feel very lonely and tiresome. But I ask you this question, if you're really wanting to make a difference in the lives of those you lead and those you work with and those you live with then what other choice do you have but by Leading from the Middle?

So, settle in. Realized that this game is played over a long period of time and influence. Trust takes a long time and consistency to nurture and build. Also realize this game you're playing is not a Sprint, it is a long-distance run that often you will not see the finish line of. Learn the value of patience, and intentional communication.

I know that seems so daunting, doesn't it? The thing is, when you realize that this is going to be more of a lifestyle for you, there is no end to the heights that you can reach as a leader. If you think that you are going to rise to some level of perfection, or that you're going to find some peak at the top of this mountain to which you'll stick your flag, I'll tell you that is a very short-sighted goal.

What you must grasp is the fact that this is an ever changing, ever molding, ever growing, ever moving, lifestyle for which every day is an opportunity to learn how to lead on even a higher level than you are already. And once you settle into that idea and that notion, you'll be able to rest easy when things aren't going according to plan. You'll realize when your team isn't where you want them to be, that they, like you, are a part of an ever growing ever influencing process.

Also realizing that guiding others and leading others isn't always a quick and easy way to go. It's a lot easier to just yell and bark orders at people than to actually try to change their mindset. It takes a consistent and steady hand with people and a great deal of intentionality to guide others to success towards a common goal.

A mentor of mine once told me "Mikel, if you're to go out into that field and tug on that horse's halter as hard as you can and jerk his head, is he likely to come along with you? Of course, I told him no. "I'm going to get all of him I want and more and there's a good chance I'll get hurt." Perry smiled and said "yes that's true. You walk out there, and you jerk that horse around and you're mean that horse won't want to do a darn thing for you. And Mikel people are much the same way. You force your way with folks, you yell and make demands, no one is going to want to follow you, and there's a good chance no one will ever believe in you."

So I ask you reader, as you have led the way in many different endeavors, were you that guy that went out and forced your way, made unreasonable demands, quick to anger, and made everyone on your team miserable? If so, I hope you change that path and move forward in an all new way.

Fourth: The next thing that you need to do is begin to recognize change in your teammates on the micro level. Any positive change as you have influenced them with your example, is worth celebrating and pointing out to them and others on the team. Remember that some Super

Bowls were won one yard at a time. And it isn't always the Hail Mary throw that wins the game.

When you recognize positive change in teammates and then you highlight it not only to them personally but in front of others you're sending your other teammates the expectation that you were looking for. And you are uplifting that team member and noticing and recognizing their efforts no matter how small.

Very few employees or team members will say that "yes I want to be on the losing team." Very few come into work that morning saying, "Gee I hope I fail." Most everybody wants to win and when they do you have to be the one that highlights it, recognizes it, and praises them for it.

Fifth: Be the hungry and humble leader. What I mean by this is very simple. In my career I cannot count the number of managers, and business owners, that were arrogant know it all's with closed minds and closed ears. They were quick to yell, they were quick to take credit for someone else's work, and they were quick to over promise and under deliver to both the customer and their own employees.

What your team, what the workforce, what your family needs, is for you to set aside your ego and your arrogance long enough to understand that there are other lives on the team. And when you have an insatiable desire to see every one of those team members win, when you realize that you as a servant leader have the opportunity to help them in both their personal lives and professional lives, then you have a responsibility to show them what a poised, what a humble, what a hungry leader looks like. The hungry humble leader is quick to take ownership when his team fails. The hungry humble leader is quick to defend his teammates when they've given it their all and still fail. The hungry humble leader is quick to give credit to others and allows his own merit and honor to be the light of his every decision. The hungry humble leader is quick to nurture, is quick to teach, is quick to train, is slow to anger, and manages his or her emotions in an even keel and balanced way.

    This is the kind of leader that you need to strive to be. The kind that allows his or her integrity lead the way, the type of leader that others know they can trust and come to for guidance and support, the type of leader that no matter win or lose, they will be there to stand tall and link Shields in the sight of adversity and not tuck tail and run. Once your team knows you're there to support them even when they fail, and you are consistent and steady when things go wrong, you set the tone for your team in such a way that they always know which leader is showing up to work that day. What I mean by that is, I've often heard people say, "Well it depends on which manager shows up." Then I'd ask, "Is there more than one manager?" No, they'd say "There's only one but it depends on what mood they're in when they arrive that I'll be able to answer your question."

Your team needs to know that you're consistent. Your team needs to know which leader is showing up to work. And when you do this, you give your team a steadiness and a resolve knowing that their leader not only has their back but is willing to take the heat with them when things get sideways.

Sixth: Be the charismatic leader! Too many leaders show up to work as the wet rag that absolutely dampens the forward motion of your day. Be excited about the work that you are doing, be excited about the people you're doing that work with and be excited when challenges come your way to test your metal.

Remember that every setback should not cause you to be crestfallen every time things don't go your way. These challenges you face show you where your team is weak, and you discover weak points, you take that as intel on where to start to improve the team.

Example: Your family is great at working in the yard. When it's time to dig in, they all show up, don't complain, and kick total ass. But, take a summer trip to Aunt Bertha's house; after being in the car together for 10 hours, and your family falls apart.

This isn't a problem, but an annoyance. You need to recognize it as intel! Data! Knowledge! Now it's time to get your team together and figure out how to conquer the challenge.

Seventh: Go back through this book and see how I approached the issues we faced at a failing sight. Live those steps. Train those steps in your mind daily. Do them consistently, and you will consistently Lead from the Middle. I will add the do's and don'ts to the end of this chapter. Lastly, I'll say this. This chapter could be 1000 pages long on the attributes of a leader and what you should do in order to Lead from the Middle. At the end of the day, what matters is your attitude and your consistency and willingness to keep trying. So don't get down, don't get frustrated, don't allow those inner thoughts to condemn you every time you fail.

MAKE ROOM FOR FAILURE! Because failure is a phenomenal teacher, one by which we all need to embrace. I want to encourage you and let you know every great leader worth their salt has failed miserably and fallen on their faces. But the dividing line between those successful leaders, and those who walked away in frustration and anger was the willingness to steady their resolve, believe in their mission, and move forward anyway.

My friend. I want you to know that the pathways of leading from the middle can change a mindset, make a losing team win, grow strong bonds of brotherhood, and possibly, save a life. So don't surrender to the path of least resistance. But rather, forge your own path and stand against the status quo!

12
ONE
CHANCE

It is 3am, and my phone rings. I kept it next to my bed because of the nature of my job. Wiping the sleep from my eyes and answer with a groggy, "Hello, Mikel here. What's up?"

In that moment, that single moment, I knew whatever I said next would mean life or death for someone that was in desperate need. Beyond a shadow of a doubt, whatever I chose to say would be received by someone at the end of their rope; they had to know it was the absolute truth. If I bullshitted this guy for even a moment it was over, and I had a front row seat to his death, not to mention lose someone I really cared about.

The rain pounded the ground and phone so hard I had a difficult time hearing William. Along with the sound of the gun occasionally tapping against his teeth, his voice was muffled. I knew I only had a fraction of a second to respond. I also knew 911 would have to be called, and we had to be careful. Trying to text, I had to pay close attention to the guy on the other end of the line. I was between a rock and a hard place and looking back, I'm certain there are things I could have done better or different but now was the time for action.

Taking pains to listen, truly listen, I wanted to hear what he had to say. I needed intel, I needed data before I said a damn thing. This man was at the end of his rope and he was just about one of the most likable guys I had ever met. I had to get this right! More than once I had seen him covered in grease and muck. More than once I had seen him bust his ass. And more than once he had swung in there for me on the job site to show he had my back. Was he perfect? Hell no. Are any of us?

Getting the depth of what was going on, my wife in bed beside me, had hands clasped praying for William. This helped, knowing that in whatever way she could, she had my back at this moment. My heart was pounding and full of fear. My head was racing with the notion of 'What if I say the wrong thing?', 'What if I mess this up?', 'What should I do?' I can't hang up and dial 911... If he sees flashing lights, I'll lose him! All the doubt and fear a person could feel, I was going through at this moment. Fact is, there was no time for doubt. I said a quick prayer under my breath, swallowed my fear, and acted.

There was finally a break in his words and I could tell this was my moment. I needed to say something and NOW! With a lump in my throat and my heart pounding in my head, I said these words, throwing the dice of what he would do when he heard them. There was not so much as a shadow of a doubt that if there was a hint of a lie, so much as a twisted truth, or flowery pleading, this man would be gone to us in an instant.

I took a deep breath and spoke. "William, I love you."

Silence. My heart sank.

"William, I love you and you know I do. I don't care what you've done. Or what happened to get you here. But I'll stand with you. I'm not going anywhere."

More silence. I felt as though I had lost him. Was he even still there?

"William, I love you and you know I do. You know I've invested a lot of time in you because I clearly see the greatness in you. Don't do this. I'm pleading that you don't do this just for the fact that I love you. I care about you brother. Even though there's the whole wide world resting on your shoulders, there's one person who's willing to walk through it with you and you're on the phone with him. William, I don't care how bad it all is, I will stand by you."

Silence.

"William. Say something buddy. Are you there?"

The silence finally broke into uncontrollable sobbing. At least with that I knew he was still with us and hadn't done anything yet. "William, can you still hear me?" I could make out a yes.

"Brother, I want you to know that you are a person who feels lost but you aren't lost. You're just off the path a little bit and we can fix that. There's nothing you have done that we can't course correct. And you aren't alone. You have friends there on that site, if they knew what you were going through, they would drop what they were doing and help you in an instant. A lot of folks can never say that. Do you see that?"
Finally, William answered back. "Yes Mikel I can see that. I love you too brother. Thank you! Thank you for

answering! Thank you for being there for me! This is just too big for me to handle!"

I was quick to reply.

"Let me carry the weight. Let Trevor, Travis, and all your other brothers. William, can you do me a favor, I need your help?" He was not slow to answer. "Yes, of course I'll help you." "Brother, Trevor is looking for you as we speak. Would you please get up and walk over to him for me? He's awfully worried about you and like me, loves you and wants to see you safe. He wants the best for you and is wanting to help."

I could hear him get up. The rain had subsided, and I could hear his steps on the gravel as he walked to meet his friend in the dark of the night. One step at a time. Each one bringing him closer to safety, all the while, continuing to lift him up and staying in his ear. He was safe.

That night a life was saved. And to be honest, as imperfect as I am, I give all the glory to God, and the guys that helped me bring William back from the brink. The conversation was much bigger with William but I have no desire to air out anyone's dirty laundry. The lovely thing about laundry is, it can be washed, cleaned, sorted out, and put away. I want to honor this man in this way. I believe with all my heart that I alone did not save William that early 3 am. I believe having some context, good leadership, the good Lord, and time did, though! I believe he saw the way that I led in difficult situations and through consistency, he knew I would answer that phone. He told me later he knew not to call the president, CEO, or our investor. He knew none of them would answer the phone. But when he saw my name as he was scrolling one last time, he thought to call me, and I am glad he did because he's still with us to this day living a full and happy life.

My friends, all the bravado and macho bullshit we subscribe to in moments like these will get us nowhere. In moments like these the person on the other side of the phone needs to know you love them and you will stand by them. They need compassion, truth, and logic. And how will they know what you are saying is true unless you've already proved it to them. And how do you prove it to them? Through consistent action, through owning your mistakes in front of them, by staying humble but hungry, by getting their back when the chips are down, by getting there early, and staying late, through integrity, honor, truth and living these things out as if your life depends on it, that's how! You've got to show them before they will ever believe your words.

I decided, even though I wasn't the president of the company, rich, handsome, athletic, or successful as the world deems it. I would still strive to do the next right thing for a group of guys working on a mountain that most folks couldn't give a rip about. That's where it needs to start for all of us whether we work in an office, at home, or in the dirt.

We must be willing to put our pride and ego aside so that others can have a better go at it and get a leg up in life. We need to be willing to put our discomfort aside so that we can know how to lead others in the way that they need instead of the way we all assume they need. Collectively as a team we need to be willing to lead, despite our lowly station in the organization and care more about someone else than our next promotion, looking good in front of management, or filling our egos with the next accomplishment.

This site, these guys, meant more to me than any job, and it was my duty to do more than manage them, but to lead them despite all the problems we faced. At the end of that three weeks, not only did we have the good graces of the site management, not only did we supersede production expectations, *we saved a human life*. To me, I don't need flag waving, I don't need a trophy, or the praises of my bosses. That in and of itself is a gift that will be cherished for the rest of my life, and I owe it all to Leading from the Middle!

My friend, no matter where you are in life, you have an opportunity to build a mighty legacy. And not one built of car collections and private jets. One of integrity, honor, truth and consistent leadership. Living life in this way will grow you, make you strong, steady your resolve, and help others to live.

I say it all the time and I think that it's a good way to end this book.

Build a Legacy that will far Surpass your Legend and inspire others to do the same

LEAD FROM THE MIDDLE

WHAT NOT TO DO:

1. **Don't yell, threaten or belittle people.** This only makes matters and performance worse. Besides, all the yelling in the world won't fix most problems and you only end up coming across like a broodish child who is inept at leading others.

2. **Don't let your ego lead:** Put your ego aside and learn to become a servant leader. In the long run people will respect you more, and go further with you.

3. **Don't make assumptions:** Yes the issues may be glaringly blatant. They might be right in front of you. But put away what you think you know and dig for the facts of what the root problems actually are.

4. **Don't give unreasonable demands:** This is where fatalities, and accidents happen. When you give those unreasonable demands and people fight to meet them, things get forgotten, misplaced, unchecked.

5. **Don't point fingers:** When problems are this bad, you don't have time for the he said she said game. It's time to take ownership as a whole, and move forward as a whole. You can get to the bottom of whodunnit later. The client needs to see action, they need to be reassured you have things well at hand.

6. **Don't focus on negativity and stay positive:** A forward thinking and moving leader puts the pity party aside and keeps their head in the game. Now is the time

for keeping yourself focused on what you do have to win and keeping your team reassured you can and will win.

7. **Don't Give Out Placebos:** As I have grown as a leader more and more I see how corrosive the "safety incentive plans," the "Take em out for dinner, that will fix everything," the "inspirational phone chat from the president," truly are. With no real change behind these gestures, you are only delaying the inevitable.

8. **Don't be in a hurry:** Slow down! Let nothing or no one spin you into a panic. You are a leader. You are the one responsible. Take one issue at time and crush them, obliterate them, and move to the next one. Rush, rush, rush, only makes matters worse. It's like being in a hurry trying to untie a knotted string. You will only make the knot worse.

WHAT TO DO:

1. **Have an insatiable desire to see everyone in the room win:** Yup, even the guy you don't like. When you realize that you are leading from the middle, and you realize in order for you to win, everyone else needs to as well, it's easier to stomach serving those less desirable to work with. Wanting all involved to win isn't enough. Now you have to make choices and act in such a way that backs up that realization.

2. **Truly Listen:** I heard it once said, "Mikel, folks typically won't listen, until they know you are willing to first." If you want to gain trust and loyalty, it begins here. Listen, learn, and be slow to speak. Ask lots of questions, and gain knowledge like Sherlock Holmes.

3. **Include Your Team In The Decision Making Process:** Too many execs do just the opposite. They sit in their board rooms with a bunch of college know-it-alls that have never had calloused hands, ran equipment, or worked more than a day on a site. Then they run some numbers and tell you how to do your job. Don't be that guy! Include your people in the decision-making process, get them involved and they will have ownership of the outcome.

4. **Tackle One Problem at a Time:** I know this may sound impossible especially in multifaceted sites. I will tell you at first, I was unable to do this as well. But once

I was able to prioritize and execute, man that made all the difference in the world!

5. **<u>Get In The Dirt With Your People:</u>** As a safety guy I ran equipment, helped maintenance troubleshoot, and replaced hydraulic lines. As an exec, I cleaned out tracks, took out the trash, cleaned toilets, talked to my people at 3a.m. Get in the mud and the muck, Show them you are willing to do anything they are to get the job done. Show them you care and are a part of the team. Show them by your example and you can't imagine how much your people will respect you for it.

6. **<u>Fill Your People with Fire:</u>** There's nothing worse than a wet blanket, doom and gloom leader! Your lack of charisma is putting your team and your production goals to sleep! Wake up! Get excited! Fill your people with hope! Be the kind of leader that inspires your people to move just a little bit farther, harder, higher.

7. **<u>Allow Them to Hold You Accountable:</u>** At Bowman Legacies we have built something called the Problem Protocol. This is an S.O.P. for communication and problem solving. One of the rules demands you don't complain but look for answers instead.

8. **<u>Recognize And Utilize Talent:</u>** Play to your team's strengths. Truly give a hard look at each individual member of your team and ask the question, "where do they strive, what are they best at, how can I make them thrive?

Suggested Reading List (ReListed):

1. John C. Maxwell: Failing Forward
Maxwell takes a closer look at failure and reveals that the secret of moving beyond failure is to use it as a lesson and a stepping-stone.

2. John C. Maxwell: The 360 Leader
Maxwell debunks the myths that hold people back from leaning into and developing their influence.

3. John C. Maxwell: The Winning Attitude:
If you're struggling with an ingrained negative attitude, there's real hope for you. In this book, bestselling author and leadership expert Dr. John C. Maxwell shows you how you can change and become a winner.

4. John C. Maxwell: Developing the Leaders Around you:
It's not enough for a leader to have vision, energy, drive, and conviction. If you want to see your dream come to fruition, you must learn how to develop the leaders around you.

5. John C. Maxwell: Becoming a Person of Influence
Learn the tactics to interact more effectively with people, and watch your organizational success go off the charts!

6. Jocko Willink & Leif Babin: Extreme Ownership
Detailing the resilient mindset and total focus principles that enable SEAL units to accomplish the most difficult combat missions, Extreme Ownership demonstrates how to apply them to any team or organization, in any leadership environment.

7. Jocko Willink & Leif Babin: Dichotomy of Leadership
With examples from the authors' combat and training experiences in the SEAL teams, and then a demonstration of how each lesson applies to the business world,—skills that are mission-critical for any leader and any team to achieve their ultimate goal: VICTORY.

Speaking Engagements

If you are looking for someone to inspire teamwork and motivate leadership, Look no further. Mikel uses real-life experience to teach principles you can easily implement in the workspace. He is an excellent choice with over 20 years' experience in speaking to audiences large and small on a number of topics:

INSPIRATIONAL KEYNOTE
LEADERSHIP DEVELOPMENT
ORGANIZATIONAL CULTURE
TEAM BUILDING
SAFETY CULTURE

Mikel's combines his work experience as GM and his experience counseling individuals with a unique perspective on leadership. He is an expert at bridging the gap between the executive staff and 'boots on the ground' teams.

Current conferences:
"Leading From the Middle"
"The Problem Protocol"
"Linking Shields"

For more information, visit our website:
BowmanLegacies.mykajabi.com
Or email us: **BowmanLegacies@gmail.com**

ABOUT THE AUTHOR

Mikel Bowman has had a career spanning from blue-collar, to non-for-profit, counseling, heavy-equipment operator, safety director and executive positions. Using his experience in these different areas, he developed pathways to bridge the gap between the executive staff and boots on the ground.

These techniques are helping anyone from CEO's to entry-level workers lead on a level they never knew they could. Helping individuals in both their professional and their personal lives reach toward success!

'Lead from the Middle' is a conference that teaches teams on a broader scale. After doing this many times over the past few years, it was decided this message needs to go further.

Thus, this book was born.

Made in the USA
Columbia, SC
11 December 2023